THE TREASURE HIDDEN IN A FIELD

JUHANI ULJAS

Laestadian Lutheran Church (LLC), Plymouth, Minnesota

Juhani Uljas

The Treasure Hidden in a Field

Published in the United States by
Laestadian Lutheran Church
10911 Highway 55, Suite 203
Plymouth, Minnesota 55441
©LLC 2003

Originally published as *Peltoon kätketty aarre* by
Suomen Rauhanyhdistysten Keskusyhdistys ry.
(SRK, The Central Organization of Finnish Associations of Peace)
Oulu, Finland

English translation: Paul Sorvo
Editor: Paul Waaraniemi
Artist: Joonas Vähäsöyrinki
Original design and layout: Elise Luokkanen
Layout: Ruth Roiko

ISBN: 1-887034-04-8
h g f e d c b a

Johnson Litho Graphics Ltd.
Eau Claire 2003

Juhani Uljas

Born in Rusko, Finland December 27, 1926

Graduated from the Turku Finnish Coeducational School 1945

M.Sc (Eng.) from Helsinki University of Technology,
Department of Surveying 1951

Worked for the National Land Survey of Finland
1951-1991, during which he served
1974–1991 as Chief District Surveyor in Vaasa Province.

Surveyor Counselor 1987

Called to be a Preacher 1956

Member of the SRK Board of Directors 1966—

Member of the SRK Executive Committee 1999—

TABLE OF CONTENTS

ACKNOWLEDGEMENTS

The LLC Publications Committee selected Juhani Uljas's *Peltoon kätketty aarre* for translation and publication in English for the benefit of North American readers and English readers everywhere. Now appearing in English as *The Treasure Hidden in a Field*, the original work in Finnish was published in 2000 by Suomen Rauhanyhdistysten Keskusyhdistys, SRK (Finland's Central Organization of Associations of Peace).

It is hoped that this Scripture-based book will serve believers at home, in Bible class, confirmation school, and in discussions of faith and doctrine. May it edify personal faith as well as serve in mission work—domestic and foreign—to help in explaining the doctrine and understandings of God's kingdom. May this book also instruct the seeking reader how to find the gracious God, in whose kingdom he can hear and believe Christ's gospel of forgiveness.

We thank Juhani Uljas and, our Finnish sister organization, the SRK, for permission to translate and publish this book. We also thank Paul Sorvo for his willing service in translating the book, Russell Roiko for reviewing the translation, and Melba Simonson for helping with the editorial process. Above all we thank the Heavenly Father for giving all the gifts that have made publication of *The Treasure Hidden in a Field* possible.

On behalf of the LLC Publications Committee,
Paul Waaraniemi, Editor
December 2, 2003

PREFACE

During 1997, at the request of its chief editor, I wrote articles on doctrinal topics for the *Siionin Lähetyslehti* [Zion's Mission Paper, published by SRK in Oulu, Finland]. The assigned topics were to be examined on the basis of the Scriptures and the writings of Luther. Edited and expanded, the articles form the basis for this book. During the writing, the number of topics increased so that this book encompasses more than I envisoned in the beginning.

Above all, I have wanted to listen to the teaching of the Scriptures. In understanding and interpreting them, I have relied on Luther's small and large catechisms and also Luther's and other confessional writings that have been published in Finnish. My earlier, more thorough familiarization with this bibliography has been a blessed continuation of confirmation school. I have not written for myself, but I have received much.

A decade ago, a door opened for the SRK for its own foreign mission work. God has blessed this work and, at the same time, He has given a new and demanding educational responsibility. Having participated in the work, I have again and again had to ask myself what is most crucial, most important, and most inalienable in my faith. These ponderings have, for their part, led me to write this book.

A guest at summer services [SRK's *suviseurat*] certainly notices the great number of young people attending. It has been harder to notice that in the crowd there have been thousands of seekers of God's kingdom, many of whom have also found it.

I have written my book for you, the young person who wants to grow in the knowledge of God's Word and the knowledge of Christ and to remain a child of God. In like manner, I have written for you, who would like to find a forgiving God. I have written also for you, who have already found the treasure hidden in a field and want to learn to know your treasure.

This writing has progressed slowly. My moods have varied during this time. I probably would not have had the strength to complete the work, if the brothers in faith and, especially the reading group established by the SRK, had not supported and encouraged me. I thank you, dear brothers.

October 17, 2000

Juhani Uljas

SEEK AND YE SHALL FIND

MAN SEEKS GOD

People have sought God at all times and in all cultures. Massive temples built long ago in different parts of the world relate of mankind's seeking and yearning for God. When one looks at these constructions, the thoughts of the Preacher of the Old Testament [in Ecclesiastes] have come to my mind. He states that God made everything beautiful in His time and also placed eternity in the hearts of the people. The Preacher adds that no man is able to find out the works of God, neither their beginning nor their end (Eccl. 3:11). Atheists claim that there is no God. Apparently, they base their belief on the premise that no one has seen God and, therefore, His existence cannot be proven. Atheists are seekers. Even they seek God. They have merely strayed because they have sought Him in the wrong way and in the wrong place.

Our time is full of distress. Fears encircle man, who feels insecure in the midst of continuing change. The insecurity is increased by the news of world events conveyed to us by modern media. Materialism appears to be the ideal that rules the world. If some system, that has been built upon it, falls, another one steps into its place. Its name and apparel change, but the materialistic world of values is retained, although history shows undeniably, that material prosperity alone cannot give man security or success. Distress drives him to seek the meaning of his life, to seek God.

Where, then, is God? Has He died, as some theologians proclaimed in their slogan in the 1960s? Many seekers have strayed. The seeker rushes hither and yon and doesn't even know what he is really seeking. The person who is estranged from God makes for himself a god of his own liking. It differs as much from the living God as the ancient gods of stone, clay, wood, or gold.

Is man's quest condemned to be a failure? It is, if the question were only of man's quest. Jesus says, "No man can come unto me, except the Father which hath sent me draw him" (John 6:44). The Word of God tells us clearly that God seeks man. He wants man to find Him and to receive peace for his soul. For that reason, the Word of God is true, "Seek and ye shall find!"

GOD SEEKS MAN

In the Fall into sin, man lost his connection with God. He had gone astray, although he probably didn't notice it right away. God, however, noticed it and went out to seek His children who had strayed. This shows the deepest essence of God, love. He could have turned His back forever on the disobedient ones and left them under the power of death. They, themselves, had chosen their portion. But God did not act in this fashion, but went to seek them. He walked in Paradise, which He had given to man, and called them. When they heard God drawing closer, they were afraid and hid themselves. It is difficult for a fallen person to meet God, even though he may yearn for Him. For that reason, man cannot be a seeker of God on his own initiative, but God must take the initiative. Man may still hear God's seeking voice in his conscience. Through the conscience, God awakens a desire in man to go to seek Him. God also has given us His Word, the Holy Scriptures, as a guide when we seek Him.

In the Gospel of Luke, chapter 15, there are three parables which describe God, who loves and seeks sinful man. The first one is the description of the shepherd, who leaves his flock for a moment and goes out to seek one sheep that strayed and was lost. Having found the sheep, the shepherd put it upon his shoulder and brought it back into the flock. The lost sheep had known how to leave the flock of its own strength, but could not return when it was wounded and tired. The shepherd did everything and carried the lost sheep back into the flock.

The second parable tells about a woman who had lost a coin, looked for it, and found it. We will return to this, but first we will examine the third and surely most familiar parable, the prodigal son. The young man had departed from his father's home. Apparently, he wanted to forget his father and home, and they did not return to his mind too much as long as he had enough money and friends. He forgot his father's home because he had such a good time in the world. But then came the trials and difficulties, hunger and distress. His friends rejected him and the world showed its true, hard face. Then he remembered the father and the father's home. The prodigal son wanted to return home. It was not easy after everything that had taken place, but his distress drove him and the desire grew more urgent.

Life's difficulties can make a person think of the direction of his life and are expressions of God's love by which He brings about the desire to seek Him. Our Christian Doctrine states, "The Holy Spirit awakens the sorrowless sinner with the destinies of life, suffering, and the examples of others, but especially with the Word of God" (Christian Doctrine 67).

THE CONGREGATION OF GOD SEEKS MAN

God uses His congregation to assist Him in seeking man. The parable of the woman, who lost and found her coin tells of this (Luke 15:8–10). God's congregation is depicted in this parable by a woman, as it is in many other Bible portions. The coin that fell upon the floor or the ground is a person who has become separated from God and His congregation. Even here, God is a working, active participant; man, himself is helpless and passive. This is depicted in the parable that Matthew preserved for us—Jesus describing a net, that was thrown into the sea and that gathered all kinds of fish (Matt. 13:47). Jesus sent His disciples to do this work. He made them fishers of men. The seeking work of God's kingdom continues in the world to the end of time. Only then will the net be drawn to shore.

THE TIME OF VISITATION

Christian Doctrine teaches: "There are periods in man's life during which God especially draws man to Him. Such a period is called a time of visitation. Most often, God calls us already in our youth" (CD 68).

In Ecclesiastes, are the words, "Remember now thy Creator in the days of thy youth, while the evil days come not, nor the years draw nigh, when thou shalt say, I have no pleasure in them" (Eccl. 12:1). The time of youth is a time of visitation. The young person's mind is open, without conditions, and has ideals. He creates his own image of the world and chooses the direction for his life. God seeks him, and he seeks God. Fortunate is he who has found the way to God in his youth and has become His child. Oh, how much sorrow and suffering he is spared!

I remember how I, myself, experienced a time of visitation in my youth. Matters concerning faith started to be of interest. I already believed that God exists, but now my relationship to God became the subject of contemplation. What does God require of me? What will be my portion when life ends? I thought of these things when I went to confirmation school. I do not remember that confirmation school in itself had much significance for me. It was more significant to me that I received a leather-bound New Testament from my aunt as a confirmation gift. I read it and underlined the portions which, in my mind, were important and parts of which I thought I understood something. I did not feel that I had anyone from whom I could seek advice, and so my interest weakened, although it wasn't extinguished completely. Later, God took hold of my life again.

In my discussions with people, I have heard many of them describe how God has spoken to them in the years of their youth. The narrators have included those, who are believing, as well as those whose time of visitation has passed without their finding what they sought.

God can speak to man even later, all the way into old age. A person's temporal life is called the time of grace, as he can find a merciful God and His grace kingdom during that time. One's entire life, however, is not a time of visitation. For that reason, it is worthwhile to heed God's invitation. We have no guarantee that we will hear His inviting voice later. The Word of God admonishes, "I have heard thee in a time accepted, and in the day of salvation have I succored thee. Behold, now is the acceptable time; behold, now is the day of salvation" (2 Cor. 6:2).

The time of visitation is not a matter that affects only one person, but an entire nation or community. Scriptures recount how the elect people of God had a time of visitation during the Old Covenant and even at the beginning of the New Covenant. The living congregation of God was in their midst. The prophets admonished them to take heed of the time of visitation. Isaiah preached, "Seek ye the Lord while he may be found, call ye upon him while he is near" (Isa. 55:6). At the beginning of the New Covenant, Jesus, himself, preached, "The kingdom of God is at hand: repent ye and believe the gospel" (Mark 1:15). He sent His disciples to preach the same sermon. However, not everyone accepted the call of God's kingdom, rather their time of visitation passed them by. Jesus lamented the fate of those cities, around which He had mainly preached for the major part of His public activity (Luke 10:12–15). He wept for Jerusalem, because its residents did not know their time of visitation (Luke 19:41–44).

History indicates that God has given different nations a time of visitation at different times. It has ended for many of them, as it happened to Israel. Our own nation [Finland] also has received a time of visitation, which has been longer than for many other nations. We do not know how long it will last. It could end when the people close their ears to God's call.

THE JOY OF THE FINDER

Jesus' parables about seeking God's kingdom also tell of finding it and of the joy that brings. When the seeker finds, he experiences joy. The shepherd rejoiced when he found his sheep and invited all of his friends to rejoice with him. Jesus explains how heaven rejoices over every sinner who repents. The woman who found the lost coin was overjoyed and invited her friends to rejoice with her. According to Jesus, God's angels rejoice over every sinner who repents. Festivities began at the prodigal son's home when he returned. He had imagined for himself a servant's position but found that he was the central person at the feast. Surely the prodigal son felt joy, when his sins were forgiven and he was once more the father's dear son.

Jesus tells about the joy of the finder in His parable about the man, who found a treasure hidden in a field. Because of his joy, the man exchanged everything that he already owned for that field where he found the treasure (Matt. 13:44).

God's kingdom is righteousness, joy, and peace in the Holy Spirit. Finding it is such a great and marvelous matter that there is joy among the angels in heaven, the congregation of God, and with the finder himself. The discovery and the joy connected with it change the finder's life and set of values. Many, previously important things become unnecessary when we have received something much more valuable in its place.

THE APOSTLES' AND PROPHETS' FOUNDATION

THE REVELATION OF GOD

GENERAL AND SPECIFIC REVELATION

God is a hidden God. The Almighty God, the Creator of heaven and earth, does not fit into our comprehension, but remains hidden. However, He has revealed himself to us, so that we would come to know Him. Our Christian Doctrine teaches us how God reveals himself. First, it describes God's general revelation: "God meets us in nature, in the fates of our lives and the phases of nations. He speaks to us in our conscience." Then Christian Doctrine speaks of specific revelation, "God especially reveals himself to us in the Holy Scripture and our Savior Jesus Christ" (CD 4).

In the general revelation, God reveals His strength, righteousness, and love, but it is impossible for fallen man to come to know God by general revelation. In this repect, the understanding of man has darkened. Apostle Paul states in the Epistle to the Romans, "Because that, when they knew God, they glorified him not as God, neither were thankful; but became vain in their imaginations, and their foolish heart was darkened. Professing themselves to be wise, they became fools" (Rom. 1:21–22).

God has given us His Word to help us know Him. If we do not allow the Scriptures to guide us, we will not find answers to our most basic and important questions. Above all, we will not come to know our Savior, the Lord Jesus Christ. In Him, God reveals himself to us, His righteousness as well as His love.

DISCUSSION ON THE AUTHORITY OF THE BIBLE

Is the Bible the Word of God? Does one have to believe it literally? Does the Bible now have the authority that it had in past times? These are some of the questions that we have heard in recent times. They tell us that the Bible and its authority are being discussed. This discussion is not only a phenomenon of the current decade. It has continued throughout the entire period of Christendom, actually, since the serpent asked in Paradise, "Did God truly say ...?"

An objective of the biblical discussion of the last decades has been to break down the authority of the Scriptures as the Word of God by depending on so-called critical Bible research. In their studies, young people become familiar with a world view, that differs from the Bible's teachings. In this way, they come to ponder the trustworthiness of the Bible. The critique of the Scriptures has attained more favorable response than before, since the modern person is averse to any authority. He would want to determine for himself what God is like, and decide, himself, what is right and what is wrong. It has been shown previously that a person does not go far with his own ability. We need God's Word, the Scriptures.

THE BIBLE'S ORIGIN

The Bible contains all that God has seen necessary to reveal to people. It describes God to us, His will and what we sinful people are like. God, himself, has not written the Bible, rather people have written it as a God-given task. God, however, has been present at the origin of the Bible through the Holy Spirit:

"For the prophecy came not in old time by the will of man; but holy men of God spake as they were moved by the Holy Ghost" (2 Pet. 1:21,22).

The Bible came into being over a long period of time. At first, its content was in oral form. The Bible was written and collected into a book over a period of more than a millennium. The Old Testament was written almost entirely in Hebrew and the New Testament in Greek. The original texts have not been preserved till our time. If some text got worn in use, it was carefully copied and the old text was destroyed. Most of the books of the Old Testament had been in use for centuries already before the canon or holy book was compiled of them. The same applies to the New Testament, whose canon was finally established as recently as 390 AD. There were two bases for selection. First of all, the writing needed to be of apostolic origin, and secondly, it had to have been used in the teachings and divine worship of the congregation from the beginning.

The history of the origin of the Bible has raised a question, "How unchanging has the revelation of God remained when it has been continually copied?" We could only achieve an answer to the question if we could find manuscripts that are noticeably older than those known at the present time. The interest in Scripture's original texts arose only as a consequence of the Reformation in the 1500s. The best possible source text was needed to make reliable translations. The original texts were collected and compared to each other. However, the destroyers of the texts had done a thorough job. The oldest manuscripts of the Old Testament were from 900–1000 AD. Only at the end of the 1800s, were parchment scrolls found in Cairo; the oldest of them were from 600 AD.

In 1947, shepherds found manuscripts in a cave in Qumran, near the Dead Sea, which included portions of almost all of the Old Testament books. The most important of them was the entire Book of Isaiah. These texts were almost a thousand years older than the oldest books known thus far. Comparison of the texts has shown that the copiers have done conscientious work. The differences have been minor and they have not affected the factual content.

Also an abundance of Greek manuscripts of the New Testament have been found. There are two texts dating back to about

200 AD, which contain almost the entire New Testament. The oldest portion of New Testament text is from 120 AD. It contains portions of the 18th chapter of the Gospel of John.

For centuries, scholars have worked to trace a biblical text as close as possible to the original. They have worked toward their goal also through linguistic methods. A jigsaw puzzle of thousands of pieces has been put together to form a reliable basic text, which has been published. It is not the original, but the differences are apparently quite minor.

No one can read the original Bible in his native tongue, for the languages in which the Bible was originally written are no longer in use. Exclusive of experts in the original tongues, we need to depend on translations when we read the Word of God. Already in 200 BC, the Old Testament was translated into Greek (Septuagint) and in 400 AD, the entire Bible was translated into Latin (Vulgate). We also have had our own Finnish [and English] Bible for centuries already. We understand through faith that God has protected and preserved His message all the way from oral tradition through the various phases of translation efforts. He has taken care that His message has been passed on to people throughout the millennia. Understanding this reveals the Bible's value to us: it is a unique book.

Due to the manner of its birth, the Bible also has a human side. The saints of God, who spoke and wrote the Word of God, were bound to the image of the world and the culture of their time. This is seen also in the writings of the Scriptures. However, the divine and the human aspects are so intertwined in the Scriptures, that there is no reason to ponder what is divine and what is human in them. The Bible is the Word of God in human words. Therein He has revealed himself, His love, and His will to us. "He hath shewed thee, O man, what is good; and what doth the Lord require of thee, but to do justly, and to love mercy, and to walk humbly with thy God?" (Micah 6:8) [Finnish Bible translation also says, "*ettäs kätket Jumalan sanan*," meaning "that you would heed the Word of God"].

The Bible tells about historical events at length. It also contains descriptions of nature, animals, and stars, but, above all, the Bible is a textbook for salvation. The most central question of the New Testament is: What must I do that I would be saved?

Some people say that the Bible does not need to be interpreted so literally, nor do its teachings hold any longer, for it has originated within the sphere of the old Semitic and Hellenistic cultures. We cannot agree with these statements, if we consider the Bible to be God's Word.

JESUS AND THE SCRIPTURE

During the time of Jesus, the Old Testament was already in written form. The authors of the New Testament tell us that He honored the Word of God. The 12-year-old Jesus tarried in the temple discussing the Holy Scriptures with the scribes. He both listened and asked questions. The teachers marveled at His knowledge of God's Word (Luke 2:46). Jesus' response to His parents is His earliest speech preserved for us. It contains something prophetical, which, for all its brevity, reveals the house of God to us and the authority of God's Word. It is worth our while, too, to be interested in God's Word and to study it.

Jesus responded with God's Word to all the temptations and enticements of the enemy of the soul (Matt. 4:1–11). The Word was so respected by Him, that He did not need to justify it or prove it to be right. Jesus told of the rich man and Lazarus. In the narrative, Father Abraham responded to the rich man, who was in torment, "They have Moses and the prophets; let them hear them" (Luke 16:29). Unless a person believes the teaching of God's Word, he will not believe, even if someone rose from the dead and counseled him. The Bible guides us in our temporal life to the way of salvation.

Jesus was critical of the scribes and the traditions, that they had drawn up to interpret the Law of Moses. But His criticism was never directed toward the Holy Scriptures of the Old Testament. Somewhat to their surprise, he admonished people to listen to the scribes, who sat on the seat of Moses. According to Jesus, they cared for the teaching office of Moses and the prophets (Matt. 23:2).

After His Resurrection, Jesus appeared to two of His disciples on the road to Emmaus. He rebuked them, as they had not believed the prophets, who had prophesied precisely of Him. Then Jesus explained Moses and all of the prophets to them (Luke 24:13–35). The examples show that the Bible was the authority for Jesus, although He, himself, was the center and fulfillment of the revelation of God. "But these are written, that ye might believe that Jesus is the Christ, the Son of God; and that believing ye might have life through his name" (John 20:31).

THE REFORMATION AND THE BIBLE

During the Reformation in the 1500s, the authority of the Scriptures became a crucial question. Luther and his friends could not accept that in the church of that time the decisions of the church councils, the thoughts of individual teachers, and church tradition had sidelined the Bible from its original position. Their position crystallized to become the formal principle of the Reformation, which is revealed in the confessional books of the Lutheran Church, "We believe, teach, and confess that the prophetic and apostolic writings of the Old and New Testaments are the only rule and norm according to which all doctrines and teachers alike must be appraised and judged " (Book of Concord, p. 464).

Luther wrote in his preface to the German Bible, "We must always allow the prophets and the apostles to sit in the teacher's place and listen at their feet to what they say, and we will not dictate what they should hear." When this formula was followed in the Reformation, it led to a second principle: "Alone by faith, alone by grace, and alone by the merit of Christ."

Luther explained graphically the general and specific revelation, "According to merits, one cannot be called a theologian, who strives to know the invisible characteristics of God in creatures, but he [can], who knows the visible and hidden characteristics of God in suffering and the cross" (Heidelberg Disputation 1518, Theses 19 and 20). He did not belittle the general revelation, but stated that one does not come to know God by it. He added that God does not reveal himself even in one's reading of the Scriptures; for this, one needs Christ, His cross, and suffering. "Who being the brightness of his glory, and the express image of his person, and upholding all things by the word of his power, when he had by himself purged our sins" (Heb.1:3).

CHRIST IS THE LORD OF THE BIBLE

The Bible is a rich book. It provides answers to many problems and questions. Above all, it is the message of Christ. Our Christian Doctrine teaches, "The principle content of the Holy Scripture is the message of Jesus Christ and the salvation that He has prepared" (CD 7). The Bible calls this message the gospel of Christ. Luther writes in the preface to the Old Testament, "What is the New Testament but the public sermon and revelation of Christ, given in the Old Testament and fulfilled through Christ?" Peter writes, "We have also a more sure word of prophecy; whereunto ye do well that ye take heed, as unto a light that shineth in a dark place, until the day dawn, and the day star arise in your hearts" (2 Pet.1:19).

READING THE BIBLE

According to the example of Jesus, it is worth our while, also, to be interested in the Bible and to study it. Apostle Paul writes to young Timothy, "But continue thou in the things which thou hast learned and hast been assured of, knowing of whom thou hast learned them; and that from a child thou hast known the holy Scriptures, which are able to make thee wise unto salvation through faith which is in Christ Jesus. All Scripture is given by inspiration of God, and is profitable for doctrine, for reproof, for correction, for instruction in righteousness: that the man of God may be perfect, thoroughly furnished unto all good works" (2 Tim. 3:14–17).

Reading the Bible is important to us starting already from childhood. In this way many narratives become familiar to us. We learn from them how God helped the former saints. Many narratives and teachings come close to our own lives, and it is easy for us to identify with the people of whom they tell. We receive encouragement and strength to trust in God's help and to fight against sin.

The reading of God's Word is a good thing. However, the Bible teaches that faith comes by hearing and accepting the gospel. Study and knowledge of the written Word of God is necessary for us, because it leads us to seek Christ and His grace kingdom. It also teaches a child of God to grow in the knowledge of God and the Savior, Jesus Christ. When Jesus fought against the tempter, He drove off the enemy with God's Word, and then the angels came and served Him. God's Word is a place of refuge. It is a lamp for our feet and a light for our paths.

RIGHTEOUSNESS OF FAITH

MAN, THE IMAGE OF GOD

In the righteousness of faith, there is the question of the relationship between God and man. It is the most important issue in our lives. God is just and trustworthy. He is righteous. There is nothing wrongful in Him, nor does He change His mind, but He remains true to His promises. God is so upright that He can never accept anything wrongful. He cannot turn a blind eye to our sins, thinking as people do, "Oh, it's not such a big deal."

God created man in His own image. He made man to be an eternal being and responsible for his deeds. The man created by God was righteous, so that in that aspect, too, he was the image of God. These characteristics separate man from the rest of creation. Only man can be righteous or lack righteousness, the remainder of creation does not have this gift. When God looked at His creation, He saw that it was very good (Gen. 1:31). Thus, man also was good. But man fell into sin when he was not obedient to, but rather transgressed the will

THE APOSTLES' AND PROPHETS' FOUNDATION

of his Creator. As a result of the Fall, man was separated from God and lost his righteousness. The trusting relationship of the child to the Father disappeared, and in its place, came fear and a need to flee from God. We all bear this poor heritage of the Fall of the first people, which is called inherited sin. Man became incapable of doing that which is right before God.

THE PROMISE OF GOD IS SURE

God is not only righteous but He is also love. He had received a promise from His Son before the creation of the world, that He would redeem man who would fall under the power of sin and death. God created earth depending upon that promise. When the Fall had taken place, the Father came seeking those who had been deceived by the serpent, His fallen children. He called out to them, because they had hidden themselves when they heard His calling voice. When He found them, He gave them the promise of Christ, Who would crush the head of the serpent. When Adam and Eve believed the promise of God, they became partakers in Christ's perfection and received righteousness of faith. When the promise given by God is under consideration, the matter is as certain as if it had already taken place (Rev. 13:8).

The promise of God was fulfilled when the Word became flesh. As man, the Lord Jesus fulfilled the will of God. His life and works were acceptable before God. Love toward sin-fallen man led Him to suffering and death on the cross. He was the sacrifice chosen by God to atone for our sins. This sacrifice was sufficient. The anger of the righteous God was extinguished in the innocent blood of Jesus. Peace was made upon the cross.

Death could not hold the sinless Christ in its power. As Easter morning dawned, the bars of the grave opened and the Victor rose. He had crushed the head of the serpent against the threshold of hell, as some old preachers have described the matter. "Who was delivered for our offenses, and was raised again for our justification" (Rom. 4:25).

When Christ had risen as the Victor, He appeared in the midst of His own through locked doors. He had tidings of peace with Him. He breathed upon His disciples and said, "Receive ye the Holy Ghost, whosoever sins ye remit, they shall be remitted unto them." In this sermon, God preserved the entire blessing of His Son's redemption work, so that a penitent person, yearning for atonement, could find and hear the forgiveness of God from it. Faith is born by hearing this sermon and accepting it. The disciples of the Lord Jesus preached the forgiveness of sins with the authority and power of the Holy Spirit. It is the great love and patience of God that this sermon still can be heard. Man can receive it when God's kingdom approaches him.

JUSTIFYING FAITH

Faith is not a deed of man, but it is a gift of God. Therefore, faith is not a merit, on the basis of which we are declared righteous, but man owns the perfect righteousness of Christ through faith. The righteousness of faith is righteousness that has come from outside of us. It is also called "gift-righteousness."

Righteousness of faith became a central question of the Reformation. According to the confessional books, the justification of a sinner before God means that he is proclaimed free of all his sins and his merited condemnation to perdition, and that he becomes a child of God and an heir of eternal life. We do not merit this in the least, nor are we worthy of it. Justification is not based on our past, current, or future deeds. It is based on grace and on the merit of our Lord Christ, alone. His obedience, suffering, and death are counted as righteousness for us.

The Holy Spirit promises and gives these gifts to us in the holy gospel. By faith we take hold of the promise, receive it, and comprehend that it applies to us. Faith is the gift of God by which we come to know Christ, our Redeemer, through the word of the gospel and to trust in Him. We know by faith that we have the forgiveness of sins, by grace alone, only because of His obedience. We also know that God considers us righteous and that we will receive eternal salvation (Formula of Concord, Righteousness by Faith before God).

RIGHTEOUSNESS OF WORKS

The opposite of righteousness of faith is righteousness of works, that can also be called righteousness of the Law, or man's self-righteousness. During Jesus' time, the Pharisees thought that they were justified by upholding the Law and the traditional statutes of their fathers with conscientious exactness. They erred because they did not recognize the depth of the fault caused by the Fall. In the light of God's Word, their righteousness diminished to hypocrisy. Jesus said to His disciples, "Beware ye of the leaven of the Pharisees, which is hypocrisy" (Luke 12:1).

Self-righteousness appears during our time in a more covert form. It does not deny Christ, but it does not want to be justified from the godless place (Rom. 4:5). The self-righteous person considers salvation the mutual work of God and man. Man must first do something to merit grace, and when the person has done his best, God fills in what is lacking from the person's righteousness with the merit of His Son.

However, God will not join man in joint justifying work, but wants to present the merit of His Son as a gift to completely godless man. Grace we even receive of grace. John says, "And of his fulness have all we received, and grace for grace" (John 1:16). In a song of Zion, we sing, "But may it not be ever touched by merits of my own; and may the Lord help us to live e'er by His grace alone" (SHZ 32:6).

The danger of self-righteousness also lurks near the believer, for on our part, we are Pharisees through and through. The warning of Jesus, "Beware of the leaven of the Pharisees," applies to disciples.

RIGHTEOUSNESS OF LIFE

What significance do a Christian's endeavor and the fruits of faith have? The Formula of Concord answers that those who intend to remain in their sins and continue committing them do not have true saving faith. Sincere contrition always precedes faith. True faith always belongs to and is connected to true repentance. Love, on the other hand, is a fruit that follows true faith. The lack of it is a sure indication that the person does not live as one who is justified. He is either still in the power of death or he has lost the righteousness of faith that he once received, as John says (1 John 3). But Paul says, "A man is justified by faith without the deeds of the law" (Rom. 3:28).

In this manner, he indicates that the justification which happens by faith does not include contrition any more than the deeds following justification. Good deeds are not a prerequisite of justification, but are a result of it. A person must be righteous in order to be able to do good deeds.

The leading thought, when speaking about justification by faith to a believer is the core principle of the Reformation: "Alone by faith, alone by grace, and alone for the sake of the merit of Jesus Christ."

THE CONGREGATION —
THE COMMUNION OF SAINTS

GOD'S CONGREGATION

Finland is said to be the promised land of associations, for nowhere else do so many exist. It is no wonder if many people think that a congregation, too, is some kind of society formed by people, members who have common values and who think in the same manner, at least in matters concerning faith. However, this congregation is not such. It has been founded by God as part of His plan of salvation. Paul calls the congregation of God the house of God, the pillar and foundation of truth (1 Tim. 3:15) and the body of Christ (Eph. 1:22,23).

In the Large Catechism Luther explains, in connection with the Third Article of the Creed, the nature of the congregation. He would change the phrase, "communion of saints," to the "community" of saints, for the original Greek word meaning, the congregation, "ecclesia," means an assembly of people. The word, community, would depict more deeply the nature of the congregation. The congregation is the community of those people whom the Holy Spirit has sanctified.

Holy means separated for someone. The members of the congregation of God are not holy of themselves or saints. On their own part, they are participants in original sin and feel the influence of its corruption in themselves. But God has called them and has forgiven their sins through the gospel preached of the Holy Spirit. Thus, He has separated them from the world and put them in unity with Christ, where they can own His holiness. They have the holiness and righteousness of Christ in the fellowship of the congregation. If this fellowship breaks, they are like a vine's dry and dead branches, which do not bear fruit. The work of the Holy Spirit must continue in us for our corrupt nature wants to separate us from Christ and His congregation.

The congregation of God cannot be seen with the eyes. The Pharisees once came to Jesus and asked, "When is the kingdom of God coming?" Jesus answered them, "The kingdom of God cometh not with observation: neither shall they say, Look here, or look there! For, behold, the kingdom of God is in your midst" (Luke 17:20, 21) [Translation corresponds with the Finnish Bible]. Jesus said to Nicodemus, "Verily, verily, I say unto thee, Except a man be born again, he cannot see the kingdom of God" (John 3:3). New birth means receiving faith and becoming a child of God. Only faith opens one's understanding to see the congregation of God in the midst of people here in time.

Luther explains the nature of the congregation in his preface to the book of Revelation, "The mind does not comprehend the one holy Christian congregation on earth." Man cannot see it with the aid of reason, even if he put on "all of the [world's] spectacles," for the enemy of souls has covered it with faults and heresies.

The congregation of God can be seen only through faith, when the Holy Spirit opens the eyes. Through faith we see as John did, "And I, John saw the holy city, new Jerusalem, coming down from God out of heaven, prepared as a bride adorned for her husband. And I heard a great voice out of heaven saying, Behold the tabernacle of God is with men, and he will dwell with them, and they shall be his people, and God himself shall be with them, and be their God" (Rev. 21:2, 3). [Translation corresponds with the Finnish Bible.]

THE WORK OF THE HOLY SPIRIT

Luther teaches in the Large Catechism that the work of God must continue without interruption. Creation has concluded, and the redemption work of Jesus has taken place, but the work of the Holy Spirit will continue until the last day. The Holy Spirit acts through the congregation. Christendom is not yet numerically full, for that reason the Holy Spirit must still dispense forgiveness. According to Luther, we believe on the Holy Ghost, which draws us daily into fellowship with the congregation by God's Word. The Holy Spirit does His sanctifying work in His congregation and through the mediation of His congregation.

As the Creator, God is near all people, just as Paul preached at the Areopagus in Athens, "He is not far from every one of us: for in him we live, and move, and have our being" (Acts 17:27, 28). God calls and awakens a person in many ways, but He justifies a person in only one way. The justifying God can be found only in His congregation, in which the Holy Spirit does His justifying and sanctifying work.

Before His suffering and death, Christ prepared His disciples for the change ahead of them. He said, "For if I go not away, the Comforter will not come unto you; but if I depart, I will send him unto you.... Howbeit when he, the Spirit of truth, is come, he will guide you into all truth" (John 16:7, 13). The resurrected Christ sent a message to the congregations of Asia Minor, "He that hath an ear, let him hear what the Spirit saith unto the churches!" (Rev. 2:7). We also ask that God would keep our ears open to hear the voice of the Holy Spirit in His congregation.

THE COMMUNION OF SAINTS

According to Scripture, the communion of saints is realized in the congregation. Paul writes, "Now ye are the body of Christ, and members in particular" (1 Cor. 12:27). The members live and act only together with the body. They do not have life separate from the body. "Whether one member suffer, all the members suffer with it; or one member be honored, all the members rejoice with it" (1 Cor. 12:26). Jesus' parable about the vine and its branches is familiar and meaningful. The branches can bear fruit only if they remain attached to the trunk (John 15:1–8). A song of Zion depicts the fellowship of the children of God:

> The mark of recognition, grant we this love preserve!
> For known by this distinction, the kingdom dwells
>   on earth.
> The Spirit's power holds us the love of Christ within—
> unbroken cord that binds us together, brings us home
> (SHZ 464:5).

Luther would have gladly changed "communion" to "community," but he did not dispute that the congregation also is a communion of saints. In the Large Catechism, he describes the congregation and the unity of spirit that rules there in this manner, "I believe that there is on earth a little flock or community of pure saints under one head, Christ. It is called together by the Holy Spirit in one faith, mind, and understanding. It possesses a variety of gifts, yet it is united in love without sect or schism. Of this community I also am a part and member, a participant and co-partner in all the blessings it possesses. I was brought to it by the Holy Spirit and incorporated into it through the fact that I have heard and still hear God's Word."

The communion of saints is communion of spirit and of love, but above all, it is communion with Christ. We live and experience this to be true already here in time in the midst of the battling congregation. This communion does not recognize the boundaries of time, but passes over them. When we read about the people in Scripture, it is easy to identify with them. Their experiences and endeavors and ours have been the same. This becomes especially evident in the Epistle to the Hebrews, which depicts the congregation as God's people on a journey. A portion has already arrived at the destination, but a portion is still on the way. The travelers who have reached glory support us with their examples, so that we would not tire. "Wherefore, seeing we also are compassed about with so great a cloud of witnesses, let us set aside every weight, and the sin which doth so easily beset us, and let us run with patience the race which is set before us" (Heb. 12:1).

THE OFFICE OF PREACHING

As a young man, I attended a spiritual gathering. The speaker at the occasion was a traveling pastor, who also sold religious literature. I purchased some volumes of Luther's Selected Works. I got them cheap as they were the last of an old printing. I do not remember whether I purchased them to actually read them, or merely to support a good cause. However, I glanced through them at home and became interested in the book, entitled "Regarding the Keys." On various occasions, I had discussed with my Conservative Laestadian friends about matters concerning faith. They often spoke about the keys and the authority of the keys. Of what opinion might Luther be regarding the matter in question?

I thought that Luther surely would deal with the matter on the basis of the Catholic church's practices. I had read church history in school and had been interested in it even. But it certainly was possible that I would find in Luther's views some enlightenment on the question that had started to occupy my mind.

I read and underlined the portions that, in my mind, were most essential and worth remembering. One portion stopped me. Luther wrote that the keys are an office or power given to Christendom by God to forgive people their sins. He based his understanding on the place in the New Testament (Matt. 9:6), in which it is described how Jesus forgave the sins of the paralyzed man and only after that healed him and how the crowds of people praised God, Who had given such authority to man. Luther further said, that God does not forgive sins in any other way.

So Luther was of the same opinion as my Laestadian friends on this, that God has left the office to His congregation to forgive sins and that an unbelieving person cannot receive peace for his conscience unless he hears and believes the preaching of the forgiveness of sins. I did not immediately go to tell my friends that they were correct and that I was in error. I did not admit that my argument, that God can forgive sins in many ways, was a Pharisaic fantasy although Luther so labeled it. It was not easy to give up my own opinions and humble myself to be a beggar of grace. My structures began to crumble and my foundations give way. I had to ponder over and over again how God gives faith and peace of conscience to a person who is seeking and yearning for Him.

GOD HAS INSTITUTED THE OFFICE OF PREACHING

Probably, I am not the only person who has found it difficult to accept the fact that God has given to people the duty of preaching remission. This was the way it was in the time of Jesus. When He preached the forgiveness of sins to the man with the palsy, the scribes became angry and thought, "He is blaspheming God" (Mark 2:5–7; Matt. 9:2,3; Luke 5:20,21). I did not comprehend the matter either until I received the grace of repentance. Only after that, have I understood that the office of the preaching of reconciliation is a deeply scriptural matter that belongs to God's salvation plan.

Paul writes to the Corinthians, "To wit, that God was in Christ, reconciling the world unto himself, not imputing their trespasses unto them; and hath committed unto us the word of reconciliation" (2 Cor. 5:19). God was in Christ, He suffered, died and atoned for the sins of men in this manner. When the spear of the Roman soldier pierced the side of Christ, the holy atoning blood that flowed from it extinguished God's anger and fulfilled the demands of His righteousness. Christ's blood did not flow to dry on the rock of Golgatha and merely be a historic fact within our reach. God preserved its sermon of atonement, so that the purity and forgiveness that it provides would be therein offered to the penitent sinner. Having arisen, Christ appeared in the midst of His disciples behind closed doors. He brought the greetings of the peace made upon the cross. He showed His pierced hands and side as signs of victory. He breathed on His disciples and said, "Receive ye the Holy Ghost: whosoever sins ye remit, they are remitted unto them; and whosoever sins ye retain, they are retained" (John 20:19–23). In this manner, the disciples received the office and the authority to preach the forgiveness of sins. The resurrected Lord bound himself to the sermon of His disciples.

This office was not received only by those disciples of Jesus to whom He gave it himself; it has been received by all who have themselves believed the sermon of the forgiveness of sins. Man is truly unfit for this duty, but God has made His child fit for it. "Not that we are sufficient of ourselves to think any thing as of ourselves; but our sufficiency is of God; who also hath made us able ministers of the new testament" (2 Cor. 3:5,6).

THE OFFICE OF PREACHING IS THE FUNCTION OF THE HOLY SPIRIT

The office of preaching is not bound to anything visible, such as the sacraments. An examination or demonstration of skill is not required of this office holder, as is demanded of one in the official outward office of the priesthood. The duty, nevertheless, has its own qualifications. This is clarified by the cited portion of the Gospel of John, in which Christ gave His disciples the authority to forgive sins. The office of preaching atonement is the office of the Holy Spirit. Paul reveals the same matter in this manner, "We have this ministry, as we have received mercy" (2 Cor. 4:1). The Holy Spirit dwells in the heart of the pardoned sinner and authorizes him as a holder of the office of the Spirit without taking into consideration education or gender.

THE OFFICE OF PREACHING BUILDS ONE CONGREGATION OF CHRIST

In the Acts of the Apostles, it tells how the disciples set out to fulfill their missionary duty. Jesus had given it to them on Easter evening and renewed it before He ascended into heaven. When the promise of the outpouring of the Holy Spirit had been fulfilled, the apostles preached the gospel of the resurrected Christ to the people gathered. God blessed their sermon and a large group believed. Luke concludes his description of the first Pentecost services, "And the Lord added to the church daily such as should be saved" (Acts 2:47).

The office of preaching gathers the gospel's believers into the fellowship of the congregation. The Holy Spirit builds Christ's church through it. When man receives the grace of new birth, the Holy Spirit does not leave him an orphan and separate, but joins him to the body of Christ as a living member.

No one can take the office of preaching out of the congregation. The words and the outward form of the proclamation can be borrowed but its power cannot. Luther reveals the unity of the office of preaching and the congregation that is ruled by the Holy Spirit in this way, "There is no Word of God without the congregation, nor is there a congregation without the Word of God." By saying this, he does not mean the written, but, specifically, the preached Word of God.

REPENTANCE

When I was a young man, I had an interest in spiritual subjects. I considered myself to be a believer, but I wasn't sure about it. I had the understanding about Laestadian Christians that, in discussion, they would very quickly turn the topic to matters of faith and would encourage one to repent. And this they did to me, also. I thought then that they certainly are difficult people. However, those discussions forced me to consider what repentance is. Although they tried to explain the matter to me, I did not comprehend it. I rebuffed the offers, but God did not leave me at peace. When His time was come, I received the grace of repentance. Only then did I begin to understand that repentance was not my work, but that of God. It was His gift, which I accepted when it was offered to me. He also brought about a receptive mind. In my case, it required time and removal of my own ideas and strength.

That event turned the direction of my life. It signified a deeper change than I then comprehended. Almost five decades have passed since then, during which the world has changed.

Apparently, people have an even more obscure understanding than before of what repentance means. Many people think that repentance takes place when a person corrects his life so that it is more in accordance with God's Word, avoiding sin and doing good. Such a self-made repentance is the building of self-righteousness. It is not acceptable before God. Even many persons, who are correctly believing, mix repentance with the setting aside of sin and correction of matters, which takes place in confession. Repentance and confession are separate matters.

SCRIPTURE AND CONFESSIONAL BOOKS TEACH ABOUT REPENTANCE

In the new [Finnish] Church Bible, the word "repentance" has been changed to conversion in some instances, but the content of the matter has not changed. God shows man that the direction of his way and life is wrong, and thus requires a change of direction. In repentance or conversion, there is not a question of checking the direction but of changing it. Neither is there a question of mere "surface remodeling," nor even of a fundamental change for the better, but of construction on an entirely new foundation. Scripture also contains other expressions that mean the same as repentance. Of them, rebirth probably has the most significance. It describes in detail what is at issue in repentance. The Pharisee Nicodemus did not comprehend the necessity of new birth, even though Jesus taught him (John 3:1–21). Do we comprehend?

When He started His public activity, Jesus proclaimed, "The time is fulfilled, and the kingdom of God is at hand: repent ye, and believe the gospel" (Mark 1:15). In this condensed program announcement are found the crucial matters relative to repentance: God's kingdom, penitence, and believing the gospel. It also shows that the preaching of repentance has a central place in the work of God's kingdom. Christ's forerunner, John the Baptist, preached in the same manner (Matt. 3:2). Just before He ascended into heaven, Christ still reminded His disciples, "Thus it is written, and thus it behooved Christ to suffer, and to rise from the dead the third day: and that repentance and remission of sins should be preached in his name among all nations, beginning at Jerusalem" (Luke 24:46,47).

The speech of Paul at the Areopagus in Athens culminated in the admonition to repent, "But now commandeth all men every where to repent" (Acts 17:30).

The Scriptures give us many examples, how people have repented when approached by God. The Old Testament describes the repentances of the high priest Joshua (Zech. 3) and King David (2 Sam. 12:1–13). The New Testament again depicts how the prodigal son (Luke 15:11–32); the thief on the cross (Luke 23:39–43); the Ethiopian Queen's eunuch (Acts 8:26–39); the Pharisee, Saul of Tarsus (Acts 9:1–18); and the Roman centurion Cornelius (Acts 10) received the grace of repentance.

Each of the people mentioned was different. Their spiritual backgrounds and the outward framework of their repentances differed. But on each occasion, penitence and the receiving of the forgiveness of sins were clearly in evidence. Also present was God's congregation, to whom the resurrected Christ left the office to preach the forgiveness of sins in the power of the Holy Spirit.

The Apology of the Augsburg Confession states that the doctrine regarding repentance should be the brightest and clearest of all in the church. The doctrine of repentance and the doctrine of justification belong closely together, for the doctrine of penitence [repentance] ought to be as clear and plain as possible in the church (XXI:41 and XII:59) The Augsburg Confession, for its part, stipulates that repentance actually contains two parts. One is penitence, or the fear caused by consciousness of sin, which presses upon the conscience. The second is faith, which is born of the gospel, the remission of sins. Faith trusts in the fact that one's sins are forgiven for the sake of Christ. This gives consolation for the conscience and frees it from fear. After this will follow good deeds, which are the fruits of repentance (XII:3–6).

Repentance, from beginning to end, is the work of God, which includes penitence caused by consciousness of sin, believing the gospel, and a new life. God calls man to Him, awakens the conscience, and engenders sorrow over sin. "For godly sorrow worketh repentance to salvation not to be repented of: but the sorrow of the world worketh death" (2 Cor. 7:10).

THE APOSTLES' AND PROPHETS' FOUNDATION

THE CALL OF GOD

A person loses his childhood faith because of sin and disobedience. Many do not even know when such a loss took place. Faith, even the faith of a child, needs care. If God's Word is not allowed to care for a conscience, the faith-connection to God is severed. A person raised in a believing home and there rooted into God's kingdom may remember how sins that one couldn't put away piled up on the conscience. Little by little the conscience hardened and stopped admonishing him. The flame of faith was extinguished. God's Spirit departed because of disobedience, and it was replaced by the spirit of the world. The extinguishing of faith is not always a slow event. It is rapid, for example, when a believer falls into public sins and does not want to repent and give them up. In this way, he denies his faith by his manner of life.

However, God does not forget a person who has turned his back to Him, but calls the person, who has lost his faith, back into fellowship with Him. The person hears the call of God in his conscience.

God calls the person who has lost faith in many ways: through difficulties in life, suffering, and the example of others, but especially by His Word. The drift of the prodigal son's life into a dead end brought him to a stop. The father's home, which he had once wanted to leave, came to mind in a different light. Many have experienced a near one's death as a reminder from God. Unavoidably, the thought has come, "Someday, perhaps soon, it will be my turn to leave. What will be my condition or portion at that time?" A serious illness can stop a busy person. The things that filled life earlier now fall into the background, and the person's relationship to God begins to occupy the mind. The repentance of a friend or a relative touches a person even if he tries to relate to it with indifference or even scorn.

God calls a person especially through the preaching of His Word. The gatherings of the believers are occasions in which the Holy Spirit teaches the way of salvation. Often the matters that were learned in childhood and the instructions of Scripture also remind and rebuke the sinner. When a person's interest in matters of faith has been kindled, his heart opens to God's Word, and he no longer wants to close it.

But borrowing words from the handbook, Christian Doctrine: "Man can, however, reject God's calling. At that time, he presents many defenses in order to avoid standing in the light of God's face. In this way, he sinks still deeper into indifference and hardens his heart. This can lead to spiritual death" (CD 69). God's Word warns us not to harden our hearts if we hear His voice today (Heb. 3:15).

Awakening

God's call awakens the conscience of man. Christian Doctrine describes the awakening in this way: "When God stops a sinner before Him, he is compelled to see his true state. He sees that he has broken God's commandments. He begins to grasp that he not only has individual sins, but that the direction of his entire life is wrong. But in addition to distress over sin, in him awakens a drawing to the Savior and a hope that in spite of all the Savior will not reject him. This distress over sin and longing for grace before God is called awakening" (CD 70).

The prodigal son awakened in a foreign land to see his sinfulness. He remembered how all was well in the Father's home and decided to return. Sometimes, repentance is viewed as having taken place at that point. If this interpretation were correct, then the redemption work of Christ would have been in vain. Repentance would be a person's own decision. The grace of God, which seeks and saves, would be unnecessary. "Awake thou that sleepest, and arise from the dead, and Christ shall give thee light" (Eph. 5:14). Awakening is not yet repentance, even though repentance includes the awakening of the conscience.

Consciousness of Sin

An awakened person becomes aware of having committed sin against God. He remembers deeds and speech that his conscience condemns as wrong. They press upon his conscience. However, sin is not only known deeds and words, but it is much more. Those individual matters are only the tip of the iceberg.

"Sin is the falling away of the heart from God" (CD 23). Having completed creation, God examined His resultant work; He saw all, including man, to be good. However, in the Fall, the nature of man was corrupted so that his desire turned to evil and he became an enemy of God (Col. 1:21). This poor heritage from the first people is common to all mankind. It is called inherited sin. From this internal corruption proceed evil thoughts, speech, and deeds, which are called actual sin (CD 21, CD 22). These deeds are fruits of original sin and unbelief.

A scribe once came to Jesus and asked, "What is the greatest commandment of all in the Law?" Jesus answered, "Thou shalt love the Lord thy God with all thy heart, and with all thy soul, and with all thy mind, and with all thy strength, and thou shalt love thy neighbor as thyself" (Mark 12:28). A sin-fallen, unbelieving person, cannot love God, because he is God's enemy. Therefore, even his best deeds do not take him closer to God. God does not presume that an awakened person would comprehend the entire depth of his corruption of sin. It is sufficient for God that man recognizes that he has transgressed against Him and that by his own deeds man cannot be reconciled with God but needs pardon.

PENITENCE

The awakened person begins to seek God's kingdom so that he can hear the gospel. The prodigal son thought, "I will arise and go to my father, and will say unto him, Father, I have sinned against heaven, and before thee, and am no longer worthy to be called thy son: make me as one of thy hired servants" (Luke 15:18,19). Repentance is a change of heart. In it, a person regrets his sins and wants to turn away from them. The question is of the consciousness of sin and not the listing of sins. "Against thee, thee only, have I sinned, and done this evil in thy sight" (Ps. 51:4).

"Contrition is the genuine terror of a conscience that feels God's wrath against sin and is sorry that it has sinned. This contrition takes place when God's Word denounces sin" (Apology of the Augsburg Confession XII:29).

Believing the Gospel

According to Luther, true contrition is the work of the Holy Spirit. (The first debate with the Antinomians). It leads to believing the gospel. In his book, "The Last Testament of the Bloody King, Our Lord Jesus Christ—An Explanation of the Sacrament of the Holy Supper," Luther counsels the contrite person, "It is the correct path that you come there, where My Word is, and hear it, and receive it in faith; then you will be freed from sin in My Word of grace." He warns about contrition without faith, "If you had all of the contrition in the world, but no faith, then it would be the contrition of Judas, which angers rather than appeases God. Nothing will turn the affection of God toward us except that we give Him the honor that He is the God of truth and grace. It is done only by the person who believes His Word." Christian Doctrine makes this teaching by Luther briefer, "Penitence without faith is despair" (CD 71).

The most important part of repentance, therefore, is believing the gospel. True repentance is not possible without God's kingdom and its preaching of remission coming within hearing distance. The important duty of the congregation of God is to proclaim the gospel of the forgiveness of sins to the penitent person. According to the Augsburg Confession, "True repentance is nothing but contrition and fear because of sin and, at the same time, faith in the gospel and absolution." The questions is of faith in this, that sin has been forgiven and grace has been received through Christ. Again, this faith consoles and satisfies the heart. It is followed also by improvement of one's life and leaving sin, for these must be the fruit of repentance. As John the Baptist says in the third chapter of the Gospel of Matthew, "Bring forth therefore fruits meet for repentance" (Matt. 3:8).

New Life

When a penitent person believes the gospel, new birth occurs: he becomes a child of God. Life in faith and the fellowship of God's kingdom begins at this point. God's grace brings about the improvement of life. It teaches him to reject godless ways and to live a godly life before God and men. Christ's Spirit awakens in the heart of one who has been helped to believe the desire for a new life and also gives him the strength for this. When sin attaches and makes the journey slow, he wants to put sin away and believe it forgiven (Heb. 12:1–2).

A believer does not become perfect; he commits sin every day in thought, word, and deed. We are both sinful and righteous at the same time. However, the direction of life changes. The first sign of this is love. The relationship to God changes to one between a child and a loving Father. The children of God, brothers and sisters, become dear. The heart begins to be ruled by the wholesome grace of God, obedience of faith, and the correct fear of God. It is the fear of a child, in which one cries out to the Heavenly Father, "Abba, dear Father." Thus begins the endeavor of a Christian.

THE FUNCTIONS OF THE LAW

God gave His Law to the people of Israel, in which He revealed His will to man (Exod. 20). Breaking the Law brought a curse and observing it brought a blessing. Neither was the will of God foreign to earlier people, for God had pressed it into man's innermost already in Creation (Rom. 2:14–16). But when man fell into sin, his will yielded to evil and he was no longer a doer of God's will. On the contrary, he wanted to silence the voice of God that he heard inside himself. Moses hewed the Law into two stone tablets so that the will of God would not be forgotten.

Scripture uses the word, "Law," in many senses. In addition to the Ten Commandment Law, the Law refers to the Books of Moses (the Torah) in the Old Testament. They also contain the ordinances of the Law, which are social in nature, as well as those that refer to the Old Testament's divine worship service. Sometimes in the Old Testament, the word, Law, also means the written Word of God.

The New Testament and the Law

In the New Testament, the Gospels relate that Jesus respected and followed the Law. He said that He has not come to destroy the Law, but to fulfill it (Matt. 5:17). On the other hand, Jesus often found himself on a collision course with the Pharisees and the teachers of the Law regarding those guides to the Law's interpretation which were called the traditional commandments.

The acts and epistles of the Apostles tell how the early congregation related to the Law. The Christian faith was born in the bosom of Judaism, but very soon it received supporters from among the Gentiles. The need arose to clarify the relationship of believers to the Law. At the meeting of the apostles (Acts 15), it was decided that the Gentile believers did not need to have themselves circumcised, neither did they otherwise need to fulfill the ordinances of the Law that the Jews followed. Paul's epistles clearly teach that Christians are not under the Law because Christ has fulfilled the Law. Paul shows that the function of the Law is not to help man to salvation, but to show him to be a sinner. The Law leads man to Christ to be pardoned.

The Reformation and the Law

Righteousness by faith and the related question of the function and use of the Law were pivotal questions at the time of the Reformation. It opened to Luther what Paul meant, when he wrote to the Romans, "For I am not ashamed of the gospel of Christ: for it is the power of God unto salvation to every one that believeth; to the Jew first, and also to the Greek. For therein is the righteousness of God revealed from faith to faith: as it is written, the just shall live by faith" (Rom.1:16,17). After this discovery, Luther wanted to cleanse from the teaching of the church all the works of man that had adhered to it. The core content of the Reformation crystallized into, "Alone by faith, alone by grace, and alone for the sake of Christ."

The Formula of Concord is the last of the confessional books. It was composed after the death of Luther. It differs from the other confessional books in the fact that it resolves doctrinal differences that had arisen among the Lutherans.

This document also deals with the question of the function of the Law. According to it, the Law has three separate functions or uses: First, with the aid of God's Law, "unruly and undisciplined persons are kept within the realm of outward order and decency." Second, the Law of God teaches all people to recognize their sins. Third, the Law also guides those people who have turned to God and have received the grace of new birth. They also must live "within the Law of God."

Now, we will proceed to examine these three functions more extensively.

THE FIRST FUNCTION OF THE LAW

In the beginning, we noted that the Law of the Old Testament also contained the temporal law of the nation of Israel. Its basis was the Ten Commandment Law. It had been given not only to reveal God's will, but also to protect man. According to Scripture, the believing person understands that society and the government have been established by God. The Word of God instructs us, "Let every soul be subject unto the higher powers. For there is no power but of God: the powers that be are ordained of God. Whosoever therefore resisteth the power, resisteth the ordinance of God....Wherefore ye must needs be subject, not only for wrath, but also for conscience sake. For, for this cause pay ye tribute also: for they are God's ministers, attending continually upon this very thing. Render therefore to all their dues: tribute to whom tribute is due; custom to whom custom; fear to whom fear; honour to whom honour" (Rom. 13:1–7).

Luther's teachings of the two regiments or governments are connected with the first function of the Law. According to Luther, God has established two types of government among men. The spiritual government is founded on God's Word. With its help, people are intended to become righteous or justified, so that by this righteousness they would attain eternal life. He cares for this righteousness with His Word, which He has entrusted to the care of preachers. The earthly government is established upon the sword. In this manner, even those, who do not want to become righteous by the Word and justified for eternal life, are forced to be righteous before the world.

God maintains this social righteousness with the assistance of the sword. Although He does not reward it with eternal life, He wants it to remain in force to preserve peace among the people. God rewards temporal righteousness with temporal benefits. The two governing authorities must not be confused or connected to each other.

The first function of the Law guides a person to societal righteousness. In its sphere, Christians also are "under the Law." We do not respect the Law out of fear of punishment, but, above all, for the sake of a good conscience. Societal righteousness must be carefully separated from righteousness by faith. Also, the most law-abiding and exemplary person is sinful and godless, unless he believes the merit of Christ as his own.

THE SECOND FUNCTION OF THE LAW

The Law promises that whoever fulfills it will be saved. The Fall into sin, however, so corrupted man that he could not fulfill the Law. Because of sin, it is impossible for us to reach eternal life by way of the Law. But sin did not invalidate the will of God; the Law continues to be in force. Its duty remained to show every person to be a sinner. Luther said, that the Law is like a "hound" that chases the sinful person to Christ.

Paul describes the second use of the Law in this way, "Therefore by the deeds of the law there shall no flesh be justified in his sight: for by the law is the knowledge of sin" (Rom. 3:20). Scripture also teaches that God's Word is like a two-edged sword (Heb. 4:12). The Law's edge awakens the consciousness of sin in an unbelieving listener. The other, the Word's edge, the gospel, proclaims to the person awakened by the Law that Christ has fulfilled the Law on his behalf. For that reason, the sinful person can believe his sins forgiven because of Christ's merit.

THE THIRD FUNCTION OF THE LAW

It is mentioned in the Formula for Concord that there had been contention regarding the third function of the Law. The comment refers to the so-called Antinomians, against whom Luther had to struggle. They approved only the first function of the Law. According to their teachings, the grace of God was taken as a cover for the permissiveness of sin and the freedom of the flesh.

The third function of the Law means that, in the believer's life, the Law should reveal sin and teach good deeds. Paul rejected this concept. He wrote to the Galatians, "Wherefore the law was our schoolmaster to bring us unto Christ, that we might be justified by faith. But after that faith is come, we are no longer under a schoolmaster" (Gal. 3:24,25). According to the formal principle of the Reformation, the Holy Word of God rises in this manner above the confessional books.

The Law and how it functions also has been discussed in Laestadianism's circles. This has taken place especially during times of schism. The disagreements have concerned the third use of the Law. This was a central subject of contention in the discussions at the end of the 1800s and beginning of the 1900s, when the New Awakened and Firstborn separated from the original Laestadianism. Conservativism retained the original understanding of Laestadianism: the Law does not belong to a Christian. Also, during the schism of the 1930s, the third function of the Law was one of the reasons for disagreement, though more covertly.

GRACE AS A TEACHER

Rejection of the third function of the Law has not led the children of God to permissiveness of sin. We have received another teacher in place of the Law, for God has given us His Spirit to be our home tutor (Rom. 6:14–18; Gal. 2:19–21; Gal. 5:13). The grace of God has come to guide us, instead of the Law, "For the grace of God that bringeth salvation hath appeared to all men, teaching us that, denying ungodliness and worldly lusts, we should live soberly, righteously, and godly, in this present world (Tit. 2:11,12).

The wholesome grace of God that brings salvation does not teach one to commit sin but gives strength to fight against it. Grace does not teach differently than the Ten Commandment Law. However, the judgment and curse of the Law have been removed because Christ has fulfilled the Law.

The apostles wrote to the people of their time many words of instruction, teaching, and rebuke. We, too, need the instructions of love contained in the gospel. They are not the Law. They are not given to us so that, by following them, we would become acceptable or righteousness before God. The instructions are necessary so that we would be able to preserve the righteousness of Christ, which we have received through faith without our own achievements and merits. The instructions strengthen and support the teaching of wholesome grace, which we hear as the voice of the conscience.

Believers want to journey as children of the light. The wholesome grace of God leads us to the light. Paul uses beautiful descriptive language, when he emphasizes the value of the gospel, "For God, who commanded the light to shine out of darkness, hath shined in our hearts, to give the light of the knowledge of the glory of God in the face of Jesus Christ" (2 Cor. 4:6). In the gospel's shining light, not even the best endeavorer will accrue merits. Our security is the forgiveness of sins because of Christ's merit.

LIFE IN CHRIST

THE SACRAMENTS

WHAT IS A SACRAMENT?

The word, "sacrament," is not found in the English or the Finnish Bible, yet the sacraments are deeply founded in Scripture. In the Latin Bible, the word *sacramentum* corresponds (ex. Eph. 5:31) to the word *mysterion*, mystery in the Greek Bible. The mystery of faith, which we cannot fully understand, is connected to sacrament. For that reason, we regard it with the timidity and humility of a child, for we remember that God has ordained it.

Christian Doctrine tells about the means of grace, the Word, and the sacraments. In God's Word there are two blades: the Law and the gospel (Heb. 4:12). The duty of the Law is to awaken man to see his condition. The gospel, on the other hand, awakens faith and gives the gift of the forgiveness of sins to the penitent person (1 Pet. 1:23–25). God has given the sacraments to those who have been helped unto faith to support them in their endeavor.

According to our Christian Doctrine, the sacraments are holy acts of the congregation, that Jesus Christ himself has instituted. Christ himself is present in them and distributes His grace to us through visible elements (CD 56). In the sacrament God's Word is joined to the visible, even to the elements touchable to the hand, so that we are assured again and again how real is God's grace toward us.

THE SACRAMENTS ARE SIGNS GIVEN BY GOD

The Augsburg Confession teaches that the sacraments are not instituted among people only to be signs of public profession among men. They are, above all, signs and testimonies of God's will toward us. The purpose of the sacraments is to awaken and strengthen the faith of the partakers. For that reason, the partakers must believe and trust in the promises that are offered and shown through the medium of the sacraments (Augsburg Confession XIII). In both the Old and New Testaments the Sacrament is associated with the covenant made by God and His people and the promise given in that connection. God has instituted the sacrament as a sign to remind of His promise. Faith takes hold of the promise of God; the sacrament supports and strengthens faith.

THERE ARE TWO SACRAMENTS

In the Roman Catholic Church there are seven sacraments. During the transitional period of the Reformation, the number of sacraments became a topic of discussion. According to the position of Luther and his friends, the sacraments were to be acts founded on the commandment of God. The Apology to the Augsburg Confession states the matter as follows: "The genuine sacraments, therefore, are Baptism, the Lord's Supper, and absolution (which is the sacrament of penitence)" (XIII:4). Absolution was removed from among the sacraments, because the promise of God was not connected to visible elements but to the Holy Spirit. The resurrected Christ said to His disciples, "Receive ye the Holy Ghost, whosoever sins ye remit..." (John 20:22, 23). The sacraments have not been instituted by men or the church, but God has instituted them.

We understand in accordance with the Augsburg Confession, that the value or influence of the sacraments is not dependent upon the officiant's' turn of mind or faith. In them, God has joined His Word to visible elements and not to their officiant's having the Holy Spirit (VIII:1).

THE CORRECT USE OF THE SACRAMENTS

Luther wrote the 1520 treatise, On the Babylonian Captivity of the Church. In it, he directed his criticism against the sacrament doctrine of the Catholic Church. With the treatise's title, he wanted to indicate that the church had fallen into "Babylonian captivity" because of its errant sacrament doctrine.

When speaking of the significance or effect of the sacrament, Luther affirms that there is not a great difference between the sacraments of the Old and New Testaments. In both, first comes God's promise, then faith, which clings to the promise. After that follows the sign which supports and strengthens the faith. For that reason, Luther states that the sacraments are not "fulfilled by doing them, but by believing in them." According to him, it cannot be true that "the power to justify dwells in them or that they would be signs effecting grace." They are influential and "give grace surely and effectively when undoubting faith exists."

According to Luther, the sacraments do not benefit unbelievers, even though they should put up no resistance to them. The lack of faith is the most detrimental and persistent obstruction to grace. "Christ says, 'He, who believes, and is baptized, shall be saved, but he, who does not believe, shall be condemned to perdition.' In this manner, He shows that faith is so essential with the sacraments, that it can save even without the sacrament. For that reason, He did not want to add, 'Who does not believe and is not baptized'" (On The Babylonian Captivity of the Church).

According to the Apology of the Augsburg Confession, it is most important to understand in what manner the sacraments are to be used. The idea is impossible "that we are justified by an outward worship service without the correct condition of heart, namely, faith. Paul rejects this and teaches that Abraham was not justified by circumcision, but rather that circumcision was a sign given as an expression of faith. We teach in the same way, that in the correct use of the sacraments there must also be faith in the promises associated with them. Faith receives what has been promised and specifically offered in the sacraments. This way of thinking is clear and completely sure." (Apology of the Augsburg Confession XIII: 18–20 translated from the Finnish version).

However, there predominates that same understanding of the sacrament against which Luther fought in his treatise, "On The Babylonian Captivity of the Church." Therefore, it is necessary for us to hold onto Luther's understanding, which is based on God's Word. According to it, the sacraments were not instituted for receiving faith but for strengthening faith. The correct use of the sacraments requires faith.

According to Jesus, living faith will move mountains and overcome the world. In spite of that, the believer does not feel personally strong. One's faith seems weak and doubts surround. Still, no one needs to think that the sacrament would not belong to him because of the weakness of his faith or because of doubts. It is precisely to the weak believer that it belongs. God wants to strengthen our faith through the sacrament and to show that His sure promises are in effect.

BAPTISM

Baptism Is the Sign of Covenant

God has given promises to people and with them has made covenants, which He has strengthened with visible signs. God does not need signs to remember His covenant, but we weak people with poor memories need them.

God made the first covenant with Noah and his sons. "And I will establish my covenant with you; neither shall all flesh be cut off any more by the waters of a flood; neither shall there any more be a flood to destroy the earth. And God said, This is the token of the covenant which I make between me and you, and every living creature that is with you, for perpetual generations: I do set my bow in the cloud, and it shall be for a token of a covenant between me and the earth" (Gen. 9:11–13).

God made a second covenant with Abraham. God called him and gave him a promise. Abraham accepted the call, believed the promise and was justified by faith. God instituted circumcision as the sign of the covenant. God strengthened this covenant by giving the Law to His people on Mount Sinai.

God made His third covenant in His Son, Jesus Christ. The Scriptures call it the New Covenant. Jesus instituted baptism as its sign. Just prior to His ascension into heaven, He said to His disciples, "Go ye therefore, and teach all nations, baptizing them in the name of the Father, and of the Son, and of the Holy Ghost: teaching them to observe all things whatsoever I have commanded you" (Matt. 28:19,20). This covenant is the fulfillment of God's plan of salvation.

BAPTISM AND FAITH

According to the Gospel of Mark, Jesus said to His disciples, "Go ye into all the world, and preach the gospel to every creature. He that believeth and is baptized shall be saved; but he that believeth not shall be damned" (Mark 16:15–16). The order of God's work is clearly evident: first the gospel, then faith, and after that baptism.

The same order appears in the familiar descriptions of repentances in the Acts of the Apostles. The Ethiopian Queen's eunuch listened to the gospel that Philip preached to him as he explained Isaiah's writings. The eunuch believed and wanted to be baptized. Philip said, "If thou believest with all thine heart, thou mayest." The eunuch confessed his faith, and Philip baptized him (Acts 8:26–40). Peter preached the gospel in the home of Cornelius and the listeners believed it; God gave them His Spirit, and they were baptized (Acts 10). According to these portions of Scripture, faith is first and it is followed by baptism.

In his treatise, "On the Babylonian Captivity of the Church," Luther discusses the unity of faith and baptism. He explains that baptism without faith is ineffective: "In like manner, neither does baptism justify or benefit anyone, but it is accomplished by faith in the word of the promise, to which baptism is joined. For faith justifies and fulfills that which baptism signifies."

ARE CHILDREN NOT WORTHY?

In Scriptural instruction, baptism was not tied to any known age, but it speaks only of baptism. In the early congregation, persons of all ages were baptized in families. This is an example for us.

Infant baptism has divided the opinions of people. Already, at the time of the Reformation, there were people that opposed infant baptism, and such continue to exist. They do not approve of the baptism of infants, as the Scriptures do not contain clear instructions on this and they have the opinion that a child does not know how to believe. Luther fought powerfully against this understanding. In the Large Catechism, he wrote, "Here we come to a question (by which the devil confuses the world through his sects), the question of infant baptism. Do children also believe, and is it right to baptize them?" He responds to this question, "That the baptism of infants is pleasing to Christ is sufficiently proved from his own work" (Large Catechism, IV:47,49).

When the disciples disputed about who was the greatest in the kingdom of heaven, Jesus took a child and presented him as the greatest in the kingdom of heaven, as a "model Christian." He exhorted them to care for children in His name and warned them about offending them because they believe in Him (Matt. 18:1–6). In another context, Jesus said, "Suffer the little children to come unto me, and forbid them not; for of such is the kingdom of God" (Mark 10:14). According to the teaching of Jesus, no one is more worthy to receive baptism than a little child.

Infant baptism is also supported by the circumcision of the Old Testament, which was performed when the child was eight days old. In the Epistle to the Colossians, Paul considers baptism to be the spiritual counterpart of circumcision, "As ye have therefore received Christ Jesus, the Lord, so walk ye in him…in whom also ye are circumcised with the circumcision made without hands, in putting off the body of the sins of the flesh by the circumcision of Christ: buried with him in baptism, wherein also ye are risen with him through the faith of the operation of God, who hath raised him from the dead" (Col. 2:6,11,12).

There is reason to examine the faith of a child from the perspective of Christ's redemption work. Christ was born as a person like we are. By sinless conception and birth, He sanctified our births. We are born into a redeemed and reconciled mankind, into the fellowship of the redemption work of Christ. For that reason, a small child believes and is justified by faith.

The opponents of infant baptism have the understanding that faith is a work of man by which he shows himself to be acceptable to be a child of God and to be baptized. But that faith, of which Scripture speaks, is a gift of God. Those who disparage infant baptism do not have righteousness of faith but righteousness of works.

BAPTISM AND GOOD CONSCIENCE

In baptism, God joins a child into the fellowship of His congregation to be cared for. The endeavor as a child of God begins there. When a child grows older, the battle against sin begins. Baptism obligates us to it. Paul writes to the Romans, "So many of us as were baptized into Jesus Christ were baptized into his death. Therefore we are buried with him by baptism into death: that like as Christ was raised from the dead by the glory of the Father, even so we also should walk in the newness of life" (Rom. 6:3,4).

According to the teachings of the Small Catechism, baptism signifies that the old Adam in us should be pressed down by daily sorrow and repentance. It must be mortified, with all its sins and evil lusts. In its place, the new man should daily come forth and rise, who shall live before God in righteousness and purity forever (Small Catechism IV:3).

Many have been preserved in childhood faith and in the covenant of baptism, but many have lost their faith and good conscience, when endeavoring has been forgotten. The conscience has hardened and has ceased to rebuke. Faith has been replaced by unbelief. God has not forgotten them, but still seeks and calls them into His fellowship. When the lost one receives the grace of repentance and new birth, he returns to the covenant of baptism. He does not need to be baptized again, for the covenant is still in effect on God's part.

BAPTISM AND INSTRUCTION

The commandment to baptize contains the duty to teach: "Teach them to keep all that I have commanded you." As parents, we have a primary obligation to teach our children and to rear them in the knowledge of God and Jesus Christ. Our own example is an important part of our work of childrearing. Children learn to value faith, God's kingdom, and the holy values associated with them, if these matters are truly important to us.

The important things are seen in the life at home. The question is not of overwhelmingly difficult matters, but for example, evening prayers, asking forgiveness, and forgiving. Times for discussion and singing are also good. How blessed it is, if the children are raised so that all go to hear God's Word, whenever the opportunity exists. Instruction in a Christian home is a two-way education. So often the child teaches us to believe. Once, my wife and I were discussing in a rather stern manner. The discussion was broken by our three-year-old firstborn saying, "Why are you arguing? Ask each other for forgiveness already."

In connection with baptism, two or more godparents are named for the child. Their duty is to support the parents in the work of rearing the child. The godparent has received a great gift, a godchild, whose life he can follow as an adult friend. He can be happy and sorrowful with the child, listen to the child and show him love. The godchild also has received an important person to whom he can turn when he wishes. The godparent also has received a duty. When the child was baptized, the godparents and the parents were encouraged to rear him in the Christian faith. It signifies in the first place that, as the child grows, he comes to know what gift he has received in baptism. The gift of baptism is the covenant of a good conscience, as Apostle Peter writes about it (1 Pet. 3:21, 22). The most important matter in our lives is to keep faith and a good conscience.

THE LORD'S SUPPER

THE PASSOVER MEAL AND THE LORD'S SUPPER

The Scriptures describe how the Israelites prepared to depart from Egypt. They had a long journey before them to the land that God had promised to their fathers. Not one of them had seen the land, but in their hearts they wanted to get there. Just prior to departure, the people gathered in families to eat the Passover meal as God had commanded them (Exod. 12). The meal included a yearling ram roasted over fire, unleavened bread and bitter herbs. If something was left over, it had to be burned. The outer doorposts of the houses were to be marked with the blood of the Passover lamb. This was important, because God punished the Egyptians the same night and killed all of their firstborn. The punishment did not touch those on whose dwellings the doorposts were marked with blood.

This Passover meal was not eaten just the one time when they departed from Egypt, but God commanded that it was to be eaten at the same time every year. This was to be done on the journey to the Promised Land as well as after they had arrived there. "And ye shall observe this thing for an ordinance to thee and thy sons forever. And it shall come to pass, when ye be come to the land which the Lord will give you, according as he hath promised, that ye shall keep, this service. And it shall come to pass, when your children shall say unto you, What mean ye by this service? That ye shall say, It is the sacrifice of the Lord's Passover, who passed over the houses of the children of Israel in Egypt, when he smote the Egyptians, and delivered our houses" (Exod. 12:24–27).

This is the meal that Jesus and His disciples gathered to eat in Jerusalem on that Passover when He was captured and crucified. During the meal, Jesus deepened and clarified the meaning and substance of the Passover meal. He, himself, is the Paschal Lamb. The wine that they drank during the meal is His blood, which soon was to be shed for the remission of sins. The unleavened bread, which He broke to give each one his own portion, is His Body. He is the Bread of Life, which is owned by faith (John 6:51). The Passover meal changed into the Lord's Holy Supper. The Word of the Lord was joined to visible elements, bread and wine, and made them and the partaking of them a Sacrament.

The institution of the Lord's Supper is described in a consistent manner four times in the New Testament (Matt. 26:19–21, 25–29; Mark 14:22–24; Luke 22:15–20; and 1 Cor. 11:23–25). The differences in the details emphasize the significance of the different parts of the Supper. John does not describe the institution of the Lord's Supper, but describes, instead, that the Lord Jesus washed the disciples feet in connection with the meal (John 13:1–17). Luther writes, "The Lord's Supper was not invented or devised by any man in his thoughts, rather it was instituted by Christ without man's counsel or deliberation" (Large Catechism V:4,5).

"As Often"

The Lord's Supper is intended to be received often. "For as often as ye eat of this bread, and drink this cup, ye do show the Lord's death till he come" (1 Cor. 11:26). From the start, the Lord's Supper firmly belonged to the life of the New Testament congregation. "And they continued steadfastly in the apostles' doctrine and fellowship, and in breaking of bread, and in prayers" (Acts 2:42). In the beginning, they gathered daily at a meal, then on the first day of the week, and later less often. We do not have to set guidelines on how often the Lord's Supper should be received, but God's Word instructs us to go to the Lord's Supper when we feel the most need. The words, "as often," emphasize the great significance of the Lord's Supper.

Luther teaches, "Christ means to say: 'I institute a Passover or Supper for you, which you shall enjoy not just on this one evening of the year, but frequently, whenever and wherever you will, according to everyone's opportunity and need, being bound to no special place or time.'...Thus you see that we are not granted liberty to despise the sacrament. When a person, with nothing to hinder him, lets a long period of time elapse without ever desiring the sacrament, I call that despising it" (Large Catechism V:47–49).

THE LORD'S SUPPER IS A MEAL OF REMEMBRANCE

In their descriptions of the institution of the Lord's Supper, both Luke and Paul mention that Jesus said, "Do it in remembrance of me." As they ate the Passover meal of the Old Testament, the children of Israel remembered their liberation from Egypt and how God had led them to their destination, the Promised Land. The Passover meal reminded the people about the patient love and faithfulness of God. At the Lord's Supper, we, for the strengthening of our faith, remember Christ, our Paschal Lamb, Who gave His life and shed His blood for our sins and the sins of the entire world.

As believers at the Lord's Supper, we can eat the body of Christ and drink His blood and thus enjoy the fruit of His work of atonement. Although we do not fully understand the mystery of the Lord's Supper, we still go to the Lord's Supper, since He has encouraged us to do so. At the communion table, we feel the presence of Christ and the strength of His grace. The Lord's Supper strengthens our faith and fixes our gaze on that land which the Lord Jesus has promised and prepared for His own.

WHO IS AN ACCEPTABLE COMMUNION GUEST?

This question was asked in my hometown at a discussion evening for young people where the sacraments were the topic. The same question arose as a burning issue once when we celebrated the Lord's Supper in the small village of Kolyvan, near the bend of the Volga River. At the communion table, we experience, especially clearly, the presence of God, His sanctity, and His love. God's Word exhorts us to try ourselves that we would not be unacceptable communion guests, who partake of the Sacrament of the Altar for their own condemnation. The Small Catechism answers the question in this manner, "He is truly worthy and well prepared who has faith in these words: 'Given and shed for you, for the remission of sins.' But he who does not believe these words, or who doubts, is unworthy and unfit, for the words, 'for you,' require truly believing hearts." Luther states in a short form in the Large Catechism, "But he who does not believe receives nothing" (V:35).

That we would make ourselves acceptable, for example, by fine-tuning a special piety, is in no wise the question. The crux of the matter is this, that as pardoned sinners, we can meet our Lord and Savior. Luther says to the communion guests, "[Weak] people with such misgivings must learn that it is the highest wisdom to realize that this sacrament does not depend upon our worthiness" (Large Catechism V:61).

As we prepare for the Lord's Supper, we often feel that we are unworthy communion guests. We can be under heavy doubts, and may ponder, "Are we believing in the right manner?" Sometimes there may be some special sin on one's mind, that he has not had the strength to set aside: "Can I go to the Lord's Supper if I have done such a thing?" Before the sanctity of God, our sinfulness comes powerfully evident. The gift of communion is also in the fact that it speaks strongly and admonishes a person to correct his matters. Confession is a grace-privilege, in which we can put away the matters that trouble the conscience.

On the other hand, the Lord's Supper does not demand perfection from us. We are sinners in thought, word, and deed. By faith, we can entrust ourselves into God's grace and forgiveness. Jesus has fulfilled all on our behalf. The holy meal gives us strength to rectify our matters. The invitation, "Come, for all is prepared," is intended for every believer.

Most often, congregants who have attended confirmation school partake in the Lord's Supper. According to present practice [in the Ev. Lutheran Church of Finland], children may also come to communion with their parents. As parents, we have the duty in raising our children to prepare them for communion. This means that we speak to the children about its significance. An opportunity for this opens if we take our children with us to communion services. I have noticed, as a father and grandfather, how the children follow the communion service with interest. Already in church, and later at home, they ask about it. We need to answer the questions, explaining that the Lord's Supper is the body and blood of Jesus, which have been given and shed for us. It strengthens our faith. We can bring even small children to the communion table to be blessed. Jesus set the children as an example for a believer, "Suffer the little children to come unto me, and forbid them not; for of such is the kingdom of God" (Mark 10:14). In this way, children learn to revere communion already when they are small.

A MEAL OF UNITY

As we kneel at the communion table, we experience communion with Christ and His family members, the other children of God. We do not endeavor alone as believers, but there are dear brothers and sisters around us who escort us. We also experience joy and thankfulness at communion. "The bread which we break, is it not the communion of the body of Christ? For we being many are one bread, and one body: for we are all partakers of that one bread" (1 Cor. 10:16,17). During the time of Jesus, table fellowship signified a deeper communion than in our time. "He eats and drinks with sinners," was a great cause of offense for the Pharisees. At communion, we experience the unity of love towards the other children of God. As we prepare ourselves for communion, matters come to our minds by which we have tried the love of our family and friends. For that reason, we see that communion guests often have matters to discuss with one another and that they ask for forgiveness and forgive each other.

The fellowship that we experience at the communion table is not limited to the congregation that is present, not even to just the congregation that is now endeavoring and battling. It extends to that entire rejoicing congregation, which shall once gather at the great communion in heaven. In the manner of the Old Testament, the Lord's Supper is the meal of those preparing for the journey, those on the journey, and those who have made it to the Promised Land.

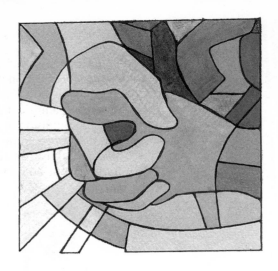

PRAYER

Prayer is a part of all religions. With its aid, people strive to make connection with their gods. Scripture informs us that during the time of Elijah the priests of Baal cried for assistance from their god on Mount Carmel. People, who have visited Islamic countries or Israel, have heard for themselves how the Muslims hold specified hours of prayer and have seen the Jews praying at the Western Wall. Prayer also belongs to the Christian faith, and Scripture encourages people to pray. Jesus gave an example for this and also taught His disciples to pray.

According to Christian Doctrine, "Prayer is the heart's humble and sincere conversation with God" (CD 78). Luther wanted to free prayer from all the formal rituals that had been attached to it in the Catholic Church. He taught that the essence and nature of prayer is to raise the mind and heart to God. From this it follows that everything else that does not elevate the heart, is not prayer. "For that reason, singing, speaking, or blowing a horn are prayer just as little as scarecrows in the garden are people" (Explanation of the Lord's Prayer). The effect of prayer does not depend on its outward form nor on our feelings or fervency. It is the simple uplifting of the heart to God. Prayer cannot be our achievement, by which we would gain merit before God.

Prayer is conversation between God and man. Man does not speak alone; God answers also. When we converse with other people, we may notice that sometimes they may not hear or may pretend not to hear what we say. Our message does not reach its destination. When we converse with God, sometimes it may seem the same. The lack of an answer, nevertheless, is not caused by God's poor hearing or our quiet or unclear speech. God truly hears and understands, and difficulties of language are not an obstacle. He is interested in us and our matters. He also answers, although it may be in a different way than we expected. Sometimes, we only later understand God's answer to our prayer.

In prayer, we can speak to God of our needs and our hopes. Scripture guides us also to intercede or to pray in behalf of others. We may enclose within our prayers our close ones, our friends, our people, and our homeland. Paul described in his epistles how he prayed in behalf of the congregations in the various communities. He also asked that the children of God would pray for wisdom and courage for him to proclaim the gospel (Eph. 6:18–20). We, too, can pray to the Heavenly Father that He would bless the work of His kingdom.

Prayer also inseparably includes thanksgiving. When we, in silence and with open minds are before God's face, we understand with thankfulness how much we have received from Him.

PRAYER AND JUSTIFICATION

From time to time, believers are criticized that they do not give prayer its due respect. The criticism is partially correct, for often we pray too little. This gift that God has given to His children remains in little use. We feel ourselves to be poor at praying. The basis for the criticism, however, is usually this that prayer is not a path to justification for us, as it is for many others.

Many people believe that they can confess their sins privately to God through prayer and that God, himself, will forgive their sins. One hears this understanding often, when we exhort someone to repent. "I do not need an intercessor. I will resolve matters privately with God." But God does not justify sinners privately, rather He sends the owners of the office of remission to preach the gospel of forgiveness to the penitent sinner.

I remember how once at the conclusion of some services, I asked a service guest if he had need to believe and receive the forgiveness of his sins. He answered, "I say the Lord's prayer every night and confess my sins to God in it. I do not need to repent in the manner that you mean." I answered him, "I notice that you believe that God hears your prayers. Every night, you have petitioned, "Thy kingdom come." God has heard your prayer and now His kingdom of grace has come to you. God wants to answer your other prayer and forgive your sin of unbelief along with all of your other sins."

On the other hand, it is sometimes thought that in no wise does God hear the prayer of an unbelieving person. Someone may even support this with Scripture. For example, Isaiah says, "And when ye spread forth your hands, I will hide mine eyes from you: yea, when ye make many prayers, I will not hear: your hands are full of blood" (Isa. 1:15). However, the matter is not so clear-cut. There are many places in the Bible, that indicate that God has heard the prayer of an unbeliever and has answered it. The decisive factor appears to be what, and with what mind, they pray. I will take three familiar examples from Scripture. They also support what has been said previously about prayer and justification.

THE EUNUCH, A SERVANT OF THE QUEEN OF ETHIOPIA (Acts 8:26–40), had made a long and difficult journey to pray in the temple in Jerusalem. He thought that it was an acceptable place to pray. There, he hoped to find help and an answer to the distress in his heart, but he did not find help. On his way back, he studied the Scriptures. Again in vain, for he did not understand what he read. However, God had heard his prayers. He sent Philip to the place to explain the writings of Isaiah and to preach the gospel. The eunuch heard Philip's sermon and believed it.

Saul of Tarsus (Acts 9:1–8), on his way to Damascus, met the resurrected Christ. Heavenly light blinded him. He, who thought that he knew the will of God and that he was righteous having fulfilled the Law, found that he was blind and without understanding. In his distress, he prayed. God heard the prayer even of a persecutor of the congregation and sent Ananias to help. Saul received his sight and living faith in his heart. He became Apostle Paul, the apostle to the Gentiles.

The Centurion Cornelius (Acts 10) prayed to God. God heard his prayers and answered him first through an angel. This angel did not preach the forgiveness of sins, but told him to send men to get Peter from the city of Joppa. Cornelius followed the angel's instructions. When Peter came and preached the gospel, Cornelius, along with his family, believed and they received the Holy Spirit.

We can conclude from these three examples that God hears the prayers of even the unbeliever, when they are in earnest.

Jesus' Teachings about Prayer

In the Sermon on the Mount, Jesus taught His disciples how to pray (Matt. 6:5–13). He warned them against vain wordiness and praying for their own merit. At least one matter was clarified to the disciples as they listened to His speech: they do not know how to pray by their own means. Many a sincere person has probably experienced this while praying. To His own, Jesus gave the Lord's Prayer, the "Our Father" prayer.

Luther has explained the Lord's Prayer in the Small and Large Catechisms, in his sermons as well as his book, "Explanation of the Lord's Prayer." In the latter he says that the Lord's Prayer is, without a doubt, the highest, noblest, and best, since it originated from our Lord. Had our righteous and faithful Master known a better prayer, He would have taught it to us also. This must not be understood to mean that all other prayers in which these same words do not appear are wrong. Many saints prayed before the birth of Christ and had not heard these words. Instead, all such prayers are questionable that do not have this prayer's content or meaning.

The beginning of the Lord's Prayer can easily slip by without our paying attention to it. For a contemporary of Jesus, it was strange and perhaps offensive to refer to the holy and righteous God as Father. Luther leads us to think of the beginning of the prayer, "The best beginning and preface is that we know clearly how to name, respect, and relate to Him, to Whom we are praying, and how we should behave toward Him, so that He would be merciful and willing to hear us. There is no name among all the names, that would make us more acceptable before God than 'Father.' It is a friendly, pleasant, deep and heartfelt address. It would not be equally loving and comforting to say 'Lord,' 'God,' or 'Judge.' For that reason, the name 'Father' is naturally innate in a person and naturally pleasing. Therefore, it also pleases God the best and moves Him most to hear us. At the same time, we confess ourselves to be children of God by that name. In this manner, we move God the most, inwardly, for there is not a more pleasant sound to the Father than a child's voice....For the person, who begins to pray, 'Our Father, who art in heaven' and does it from the bottom of his heart, confesses that he has a Father and that this Father is in Heaven."

Almost half a century ago, I sat in church one winter evening. The congregation evening's topic was prayer, on which three clergymen spoke. In two speeches, prayer became a means of justification. The words, "Our Father who art in heaven," were the text for the second speech. The third speaker rose to the pulpit and read a text that was even shorter than the preceding one, "Our Father, Amen." Beginning with these words, he led the listeners to see what had had to happen so that we are able to pray, "Our Father." How great was the love of the Father, that He gave His only Son for the remission of sin. In place of prayer, another way to justification opened. Prayer was revealed as a great gift, the secure and trusting discussion of a child with a Father who loves him.

THY WILL BE DONE

Our prayers are often about distress, oppression, difficulties, and the obvious hopes and desires that arise from them. There is nothing wrong in this, for a child has permission to speak freely to his Father. However, in the Lord's Prayer Jesus sets the needs in priority and brings a new dimension to prayer. He instructs us to ask, "Thy will be done." This is not always easy.

Jesus did not only teach in this manner, but also set an example in Gethsemane. The most important and critical events of His life were before Him. The cross, suffering, and death awaited him. More frightening, before Him rose the fact that the Father would cast upon Him the sins of the entire world and, for a moment, would turn His back upon Him. In this situation, one more difficult than we can possibly imagine, Jesus prayed, "O my Father, if it be possible, let this cup pass from me: nevertheless, not as I will, but as thou wilt" (Matt. 26:39). Jesus' example leads us to the correct humility and childlike trust. The Father knows what is best for us, even when it is difficult for us to be therein content.

"Humble yourselves therefore under the mighty hand of God, that he may exalt you in due time: casting all your cares upon him: for he careth for you" (1 Pet. 5:6,7).

THE ENDEAVOR OF FAITH

CHRISTIAN DOCTRINE TEACHES US ABOUT ENDEAVORING

"In the life of a Christian is God's peace and joy, but also weakness of faith, temptations, and oppression. God guides His own along the narrow way of the cross. With sufferings, He wishes to try their faith, keep them humble, and draw them into ever closer fellowship with Him. God also often sees His children worthy to confess their faith by their suffering. When a Christian remains in God's hands, his life is supported by an ever deepening confidence that God leads everything for his best benefit. Humble thanks fills his heart because God has been patient to care for him, who is worthless, as His child. The hope of the coming glory also becomes more and more vivid to him. Watching and praying he awaits the final fulfillment of salvation" (CD 84).

The Endeavor Is God's Work

Scripture often depicts a believing person's life and endeavor as a journey and being on the road. The traveler wants to reach his destination. To achieve this, it is necessary to travel on the right road without turning back and tiring on the way. Isaiah encouraged the Old Testament believers who were journeying amid the trials of forced captivity, "And a highway shall be there, and a way, and it shall be called the way of holiness; the unclean shall not pass over it; but it shall be for those: the wayfaring men, though fools, shall not err therein" (Isa. 35:8). When Paul stood before Governor Felix, accused of starting a rebellion, he confessed his faith, "But this I confess unto thee, that after the way which they call heresy, so worship I the God of my fathers, believing all things which are written in the law and the prophets" (Acts 24:14).

In His farewell speech, Jesus said that He was going soon to the Father, but that the disciples need not be concerned, for they also knew the way there. Still, the disciples were not sure where it was that Jesus was going and, therefore, did not know the way, either. For that reason, Thomas demanded an additional explanation and Jesus answered, "I am the way, the truth, and the life" (John 14:6). This is the core of one's endeavor. The endeavor is not of our doing or achievement, on which basis we would attain eternal life. If it were so, our salvation would depend upon us and would no longer be a gift of God. Fortunately, it is not so. By grace, we have become partakers of God's love and Christ's righteousness. We have received this through faith, which God has effected. Faith is being in the righteousness of Christ and living in forgiveness every moment. We endeavor to preserve this treasure.

There are powers around us that would want to wrest it from us. For that reason, the admonition of the resurrected Christ is meant for us, "Hold that fast which thou hast, that no man take thy crown" (Rev. 3:11). Paul instructs, "As ye have therefore received Christ Jesus the Lord, so walk ye in him" (Col. 2:6). Therefore, we are not endeavoring by our own strength, but by the influence of God's Spirit. When Paul encouraged the Philippians to a steadfast endeavor in faith, he also revealed with whose strength the children of God endeavor,

"Wherefore, my beloved…work out your own salvation with fear and trembling: for it is God which worketh in you both to will and to do of his good pleasure" (Phil. 2:12,13). Christ's Spirit dwells in our hearts through faith and works the will and the doing in us.

THE ENDEAVORER IS A CONTESTANT

Endeavoring is an archaic word. It is generally used only in discussion about matters concerning faith. In modern speech we speak about competing. Therefore, believers are competitors. The competition is lifelong. One who drops out of the race will never win, whatever the reasons for his dropping out may be. Already during Bible times, in Greece they had arranged Olympic Games, whose program included races of various lengths, throwing the discus, wrestling, and boxing. When Paul advised people to endeavor in faith, he compared a believer to an athlete competing in the Olympics (1 Cor. 9:24–27).

Paul certainly did not encourage the young men to participate in the Olympics, for they were part of the heathen religious practice which the Christian's had rejected. He only took an example from an event which was as familiar to the Greeks as the modern Olympics are to us. He invited the young men to enter a more noble contest that lasted an entire lifetime. The runner practices self-discipline so that he would win the prize, and the boxer fights with a definite purpose, and not by flailing the air. The crucial matters of endeavoring in faith are emphasized in Paul's teaching. In the Olympics, the best contestant won and received the prize, which was a crown of laurel. In the endeavor of faith, every one who reaches the end will win and receive a crown. It will not wither or perish, as in the Olympics, but be everlasting. The contestant practices self-discipline because he wants to win. He has a clear goal, which guides his entire life.

THE ENDEAVOR IS A BATTLE

When Paul also compared the endeavoring person to a boxer, he exposed the other side of endeavoring. There, where the runner concentrates on his running and strives purposefully for the victor's prize, the boxer must struggle with and overcome his adversary. The endeavor of faith is a battle also. Who are the opponents of a Christian in his endeavor toward victory? The familiar phrase from the Catechism answers this question, "We have warfare against a threefold enemy, the devil, the world, and our own flesh." The warfare becomes difficult because our own corrupt nature is in league with the opponents of God. We cannot flee from the battle nor withdraw into a fort against our enemies, for the front line of the battle goes right through our own heart. There we fight the hottest and most painful battles.

We need weapons for battle. Paul described the weaponry of the Christian in his Epistle to the Ephesians (6:10–17). He first reminded them by what strength we are fighting, "Finally, my brethren, be strong in the Lord, and in the power of his might." Then he admonished them to put on armor, so that the attacks of the enemy of the soul would bounce off of them, "Put on the whole armor of God, that ye may be able to stand against the wiles of the devil." War veterans have described how, during continuing battles, they cared for their equipment because they needed it. On the other hand, during a stationary war, when often the concern was just to be on watch, the equipment tended to be forgotten. Who wanted to carry a dangling gas mask or helmet when there appeared to be no need for them?

This can happen in spiritual warfare, also. However, there is no room to lull oneself into false security. We need all of our equipment because the enemy uses surprise attacks. "Stand therefore, having your loins girt about with truth, and having on the breastplate of righteousness; and your feet shod with the preparation of the gospel of peace; above all, taking the shield of faith, wherewith ye shall be able to quench all the fiery darts of the wicked. And take the helmet of salvation, and the sword of the Spirit, which is the word of God." The other equipment is for defense; only the sword, God's Word, is fitting also for attack. We do not fight with the arm of the flesh, but with God's Word. Jesus, himself, gave an example of this. When the enemy of the soul tempted Him, He overcame the temptations with God's Word.

From under the Cross to under the Crown

The endeavor is following Christ. He teaches, "And he that taketh not his cross, and followeth after me, is not worthy of me" (Matt. 10:38). The endeavor unavoidably includes bearing the cross of Christ. What does this symbolic teaching of Jesus mean?

Crucifixion was a cruel form of condemnation to death that was in wide use in Jesus' time. The condemned person had to carry the crosspiece and the sign on which the bases of his judgment were written. Jesus had to personally experience this. His followers travel the way that their Master has laid out.

Carrying the cross signifies first to confess that we cannot reach our destination, eternal life, at all by our own endeavor, but that the cross of Christ is our only hope. He has atoned for our sins with His blood and thus opened the road all the way to the destination. The sermon of reconciliation, the gospel of the forgiveness of sins, brings the power of the victory of Christ's Resurrection to our weakness on the way of the cross. To Paul, the prior doer of the deeds of the Law and great apostle to the Gentiles, the cross of Christ was his only reason for pride, "But God forbid that I should glory, save in the cross of our Lord Jesus Christ, by whom the world is crucified unto me, and I unto the world" (Gal. 6:14).

Second, carrying the cross means that, like Paul, we have crucified our flesh with its lusts and desires. The follower of Christ cannot follow the desires and wishes of his flesh when they battle against God's Word and the conscience. This causes many battles, as has been stated previously.

Third, carrying the cross signifies the opening of a boundary between Christ's followers and the world. At the time of Jesus and the early congregation, the believers had to separate from Judaism. The author of the Epistle to the Hebrews instructed his brothers and sisters, "Let us go forth therefore unto him without the camp, bearing his reproach. For here have we no continuing city, but we seek one to come" (Heb. 13:13,14). They did not separate themselves of their own initiative, but when God's time had come, they were shut out of the synagogue community. In his time, Luther experienced the same along with his brothers in faith. We have experienced a great blessing from God that we have been able to believe and to do the work of God's kingdom in fellowship with our nation's [Finland's] church. In spite of all this, we feel that the cross of Christ separates us to "outside the camp."

Trials become familiar to us on this way. God strengthens our faith with them and teaches us patience. If we did not have patience, we would become discouraged encountering our first adversity and our endeavor would remain unfinished. Patience is especially necessary when we stumble and notice that we haven't become good and exemplary endeavorers. We continue to be weak, and corruption affects and lives in us. Patience is required when it becomes clear that our endeavor is not the reason and basis for our salvation. We must return again and again to the place where our journey of endeavor began. To the place where the Lord Jesus is the only reason for our salvation and that we, although unsuccessful, have the right to believe our sins forgiven in His name and blood. Even Paul, in his endeavor of faith, had come to know his weaknesses. We can join with him to say, "Therefore I take pleasure in infirmities—for Christ's sake: for when I am weak, then am I strong" (2 Cor. 12:10).

CONFESSING FAITH

At the same time, when Jesus taught His disciples to follow Him under the cross, He spoke of confessing faith, "Whosoever therefore shall confess me before men, him will I confess also before my Father which is in heaven. But whosoever shall deny me before men, him will I also deny before my Father which is in heaven" (Matt. 10:32,33). Confessing faith is firmly associated with following Christ and one's endeavor in faith. No one can be a believer secretly. The New Testament relates of such people, who tried to believe in Jesus secretly (John 12:42,43, 19:38). They did not want to be labeled or to carry the cross of Christ. The New Testament, in any case, does not relate that they would have reached the destination as victors.

In practice, confession of Christ takes place through speech as well as life. It is not forced or contract work. When we confess ourselves to be followers of Christ, we do not gain merits nor do we become better Christians, but it frees us from the slavery of the world and supports us in our endeavor of faith. God's children feel themselves to be timid and weak confessors. Precisely for this reason, they often have doubts of their own faith. Correct confession is not the expression of one's own strength, but as Peter states, "But sanctify the Lord God in your hearts: and be ready always to give an answer to every man that asketh you a reason of the hope that is in you, with meekness and fear" (1 Pet. 3:15).

I have heard of a believing man, who worked in a factory. He was troubled by the fact that he had so poorly confessed his faith to his coworkers. He lamented of his weakness often to the other believers. However, once one of his coworkers went to speak to their supervisor and asked that he would be moved to another job. He could no longer stand to be in the same job with that man, for unknowingly he constantly preached with his life. The confession of Christ through one's life is not outward righteousness which approaches self-piety, but it is simply living as one believes.

SET ASIDE ALL SIN AND BURDEN

What would it feel like to run a marathon with a heavy backpack? Most likely the runner would drop out. Especially if stones were added to the backpack now and then. On the racetrack of faith, this can happen to a runner. The conscience collects sin, matters over which the conscience rebukes and reminds. The journey becomes burdensome and slow, and fatigue weighs heavily. Those Hebrews, too, were tired in their faith, to whom it was once written, "Wherefore, seeing we also are compassed about with so great a cloud of witnesses, let us lay aside every weight, and the sin which doth so easily beset us, and let us run with patience the race that is set before us" (Heb. 12:1). The putting away of sin is confession. Through it, we can remove the backpack. In the following chapter, we will discuss confession more broadly, so in this context, I only refer to this grace privilege.

The endeavor of faith can be slowed also by a burden that of itself is not sin. The trials and sorrows of life are such. There is reason to discuss them with another believer so they would not become an obstruction to faith, but that the endeavoring one would receive strength to take them from the hand of the Heavenly Father. Jesus teaches in His Sermon on the Mount that we need not worry about the morrow because our Heavenly Father takes care of us (Matt. 6:25–32). Peter exhorts, "Cast all your care upon him; for he careth for you" (1 Pet. 5:7).

WE DO NOT ENDEAVOR ALONE

In the previous section, we examined the endeavor from the viewpoint of an individual Christian. However, we are not isolated endeavoring persons, but we belong to a battling and endeavoring congregation. We would not last long alone, but God has united us in the fellowship of His congregation to partake of all the instructions of grace. They are part of the equipment which we need in our endeavor. The competitor and the fighter need nourishment so that they will have strength, for "an army marches on its stomach." Fellowship of the congregation means that "we do not despise the sermon and God's Word, but we keep it holy, and willingly hear and learn it," as the Small Catechism teaches us. The services of God's children are important to us. At services we receive the food which we need while we endeavor. In the fellowship of God's children, we can also hear the gospel of the forgiveness of sins, which frees our consciences of useless ballast.

Among the children of God we have also those closest brothers and sisters whom God has given us as escorts. We can speak to them when it feels that, "I do not have strength any longer," or "I do not understand what I should do in this difficult and problematic situation."

I SHALL BE WITH YOU

The Old Testament tells us about the journey of the children of Israel from bondage in Egypt to the Promised Land. At the same time, it symbolically depicts the journey of God's people to that land which God has prepared for His children. When the people traveled in the desert, a pillar of cloud moved ahead of them by day and a pillar of fire by night. Thus, God assured His people that He travels with them. Matthew tells us that the last words of the Resurrected Christ, before He ascended into heaven, were, "Lo, I am with you alway, even unto the end of the world" (Matt. 28:20). For an endeavoring person who is weak in himself, it is comforting to know that the Good Shepherd, who gave His life for His sheep, still journeys with and leads His own. With His blood, He has opened the way to the destination.

CONFESSION

Sometimes, one hears people admiring confession in the Catholic Church and then asking why confession is not used in the Lutheran Church. This probably stems from the fact that little is said about confession and apparently, it is used even less. Confession, however, does belongs to and is part of the doctrine of the Evangelical Lutheran Church. Among Conservative Laestadians, confession is practiced, and it is spoken of in sermons.

The believer's endeavor is a battle against the enemy of the soul, the world and one's own flesh. In this warfare, we suffer losses and are wounded. Sin attaches and wounds the conscience. To help us, God has given confession wherein we can free our conscience from exhausting burdens and to salve our wounds. "Let us set aside every weight, and the sin which doth so easily beset us" (Heb. 12:1). Confession is for remaining in faith, not for entering faith, as the original Lutheran formula for confession teaches.

What Is Confession?

At the end of the Large Catechism there is, "A Brief Exhortation to Confession." In it, Luther discusses confession broadly. He condemns the Catholic Church's confession practices. Therein confession was a work forced onto a person under threat of falling into a mortal sin. By this confession one merited forgiveness. The primary emphasis was to give as detailed an account of one's sins as possible. For his part, Luther emphasized the voluntary nature of confession. Force or fear does not drive us to confession. We confess of our own will, because we feel confession to be a gift given to us by God. It comforts and encourages our consciences. According to Luther's understanding, absolution already is confession, although it may not include any special confession of sins. He emphasizes, especially, that the preaching of forgiveness and hearing it are the most important part of confession.

Regarding confession the Smalcald Articles teach: "Since absolution or the power of the keys, which was instituted by Christ in the Gospel, is a consolation and help against sin and a bad conscience, confession and absolution should by no means be allowed to fall into disuse in the church, especially for the sake of timid consciences and for the sake of the untrained young people who need to be examined and instructed in Christian doctrine." The Augsburg Confession states, "About confession, our congregations teach that private absolution is to be preserved in the congregations, although the enumeration of all sins is not essential in confession. It is even impossible according to the Psalmist: 'Who can discern his errors?'" (Ps. 19:12) [Literal translation from the Smalcald Articles in Finnish].

According to the Small Catechism, confession consists of two parts, "One is, that we confess our sins. The other is that we receive absolution or forgiveness from the confessor as from God himself, by no means doubting but firmly believing that our sins are thereby forgiven before God in heaven." In addition, the Small Catechism teaches that before God, we should acknowledge that we are guilty of all manner of sins, even those of which we are not aware. We do this, for example, in the Lord's Prayer. Before the confessor, however, we should confess only those sins of which we have knowledge and feel in our heart.

According to Luther, general confession takes place when the congregation confesses its sins together. This takes place at a worship service and in communion. A confession of love is what takes place when we ask forgiveness of our neighbor for our offenses, whether word or deed. The third form of confession is public confession. In it, we confess our transgressions publicly and ask for forgiveness from the congregation. The fourth form is private confession, in which we confess our sins to a confessor-father privately and receive absolution. When we speak of confession, we generally mean private confession.

SCRIPTURE AND CONFESSION

Confession has firm foundations in Scripture. In Psalm 32, David describes his experiences when he had fallen into sin, "Blessed is the man unto whom the Lord imputeth not iniquity, and in whose spirit there is no guile. When I kept silence, my bones waxed old through my roaring all the day long. For day and night thy hand was heavy upon me: my moisture is turned into the drought of summer. Selah. I acknowledged my sin unto thee, and mine iniquity have I not hid. I said, I will confess my transgressions unto the Lord; and thou forgavest the iniquity of my sin" (Ps. 32:2–5). When he confessed his sins, he felt that he was before God and not before men. David also experienced the blessing of confession: the Lord no longer reproached him of sin, but there was joy and peace in his heart.

James teaches, "Confess your faults one to another, and pray one for another, that ye may be healed" (James 5:16). John writes, "If we say that we have no sin, we deceive ourselves, and the truth is not in us. If we confess our sins, he is faithful and just to forgive our sins, and to cleanse us from all unrighteousness" (1 John 1:8,9).

While discussing confession, Christian Doctrine (CD 71) points to the place in the Gospel of John, where the resurrected Savior appears to His own and gives them the office of the Holy Spirit to proclaim the forgiveness of sins (John 20:22–23). The most important part of confession, absolution, links confession to the office of the Holy Spirit. True confession can take place only in the living congregation of God. The most important characteristic of a confessor-father is that he is a believer.

PRIVATE CONFESSION AND PUBLIC CONFESSION

Sometimes one hears the argument that public confession is more effective than private confession. However, the matter is not so, because the main emphasis in confession is not in the confession of sins but in the absolution of sins. The gospel of the forgiveness of sins is just as powerful and effective in private confession as in public confession. With the wrong emphasis, we make confession into an accomplishment, by which a person attempts to earn merit before God. The shame connected with public confession adds to the merit seeking. The gift changes into a requirement.

The effect of confession does not depend at all on whether it is done privately to a confessor-father or publicly before a congregation. The effect of the confession is in the word of absolution, which is proclaimed by an individual person or by an assembled congregation together. In both instances, the question is of the same word of the Holy Spirit, that enlivens and gives strength. Jesus has said of this, "And I will give unto thee the keys of the kingdom of heaven: and whatsoever thou shalt bind on earth shall be bound in heaven; and whatsoever thou shalt loose on earth shall be loosed in heaven" (Matt. 16:19).

Among Conservative Laestadians, it has been understood regarding public confession that matters are corrected as to the extent that offense has been caused. In private confession, matters may come out that we correct more broadly. The gospel preached by the confessor-father conveys the power of forgiveness to correct the matters. This takes place when, for example, one has caused an offense against another person or the government.

CONFESSION CONSISTS OF TWO PARTS

Luther teaches, "As I have often said, that confession consists of two parts. The first is my work and act, when I lament my sin and desire comfort and restoration for my soul. The second is a work which God does, when he absolves me of my sins through a word placed in the mouth of a man. This is the sur-passingly grand and noble thing which makes confession so wonderful and comforting" (Large Catechism, A Brief Exhortation to Confession).

The danger exists that the emphasis will shift to our con-fession and to a precise enumeration of our sins. Then the absolution, God's response, goes almost unnoticed. Confes-sion becomes our own accomplishment by which we become better Christians. Without noticing, we fall under the Law. When we do not feel joy and freedom after confession, we think that our confession was not sufficiently detailed and that it should be expanded. Thus, we get into a confession spiral, with the result that the freedom and joy of a Christian disappear from our lives. Our gaze is no longer directed toward Christ, the initiator and finisher of our faith, but inward into our own selves, from which we seek the foundations of faith. However, they are not found there.

Again, if the word of absolution proclaimed with the authority of the Holy Spirit by the confessor-father remains the most central and most important part of our confession, we experience freedom from the sins that have oppressed our conscience. Confession is then the gift of God and the grace privilege that He has intended it to be.

The section in the Augsburg Confession explaining con-fession concludes: "Nevertheless, confession is retained among us on account of the great benefit of absolution and because it is otherwise useful to consciences" (XXV). The mention of sins is part of confession because we want to be freed of the sins which burden our consciences. We know that we are before the face of God and we do not want to deceive or embellish matters. In spite of everything, our confession is always imper-fect. However, the absolution is perfect: all of our sins are forgiven and our consciences are freed from their burdens.

What Keeps Us from Confessing?

Although I know that confession has been given to assist me, it is not easy for me to make a confession. The reason can be found in my supposed honor. It feels that no one else could have fallen into sins of this nature. If I speak of them, the confessor-father will not understand me and will not consider me as a believer after that. And what if I do not speak to anyone about my fall, but attempt to believe the matter, that especially weighs upon my conscience, forgiven from the general preaching of the gospel? From my own experience, I can say that one does not receive peace and freedom by this means. No matter how much I have tried to believe, that known matter has always reminded me of its existence. It has been like a stone in my shoe, making travel difficult. Then, when I have spoken of the matters pressing upon my conscience to a confessor-father, I have been surprised. First of all, the confessor-father has understood, and nothing implied that he did not consider me a believer. When, in God's behalf, he has proclaimed all sins forgiven in the name and blood of Jesus, I have experienced liberation. The faults, which gave me pain, no longer rose accusingly to mind. The stone has been taken away, and the travel feels easy. I have only regretted that I have carried burdens on my conscience in vain.

I have been a confessor-father, also. The believers, who have related about their matters and whom I have been able to comfort with the words of release, have become close and dear. I have not considered them poor in their endeavor. I have learned to know them as Christians, for whom the matter of faith is important and who endeavor to retain faith in a good conscience. I also know, that as a confessor-father, I have an unconditional responsibility to remain silent.

Therefore, confession is a God-given gift to us, that helps us in our endeavor of faith. We go to make confession just as much a believer as when we return. The word of absolution, that belongs to confession has simply freed our consciences from heavy burdens. The performance of confession does not cleanse our consciences, but belief in the word of absolution. God does not cleanse our hearts by confession, but by faith (Acts 15:9). Luther concludes the above-mentioned exhortation to confession thusly, "Therefore, when I urge you to go to confession, I am simply urging you to be a Christian."

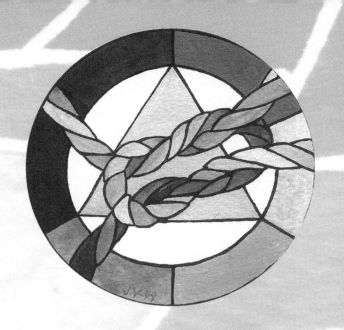

TIME AND ETERNITY

CITIZENS OF TWO KINGDOMS

NATIONS AND CITIZENSHIP

There are many kingdoms in the world. Their people are citizens of those homelands. They have rights and obligations. If someone moves permanently to live in another land, he can apply for its citizenship. If he receives it, he usually forfeits the citizenship of his former homeland. Some countries', for example the USA's, citizenship is especially sought after. Also the citizenship of ancient Rome was sought after: all did not have it. Paul had it, and he referred to it in a situation where he especially needed the legal security it provided, "civis romanus sum," or "I am a citizen of Rome."

Usually a person can only be a citizen of one kingdom, enjoy its rights, and be bound by its obligations. There are few exceptions to this rule. One of these is that in addition to our homeland, we can be citizens of God's kingdom. Pilate asked Jesus, "Art thou King of the Jews?" Jesus answered kingdom is not of this world." The boundaries of God's king-dom have not been drawn on any map, nor can its boundaries be found on the land. However, boundaries do exist. They run through hearts. For that reason, one can be a citizen of two nations: his homeland and God's kingdom. God's kingdom is hidden, it is seen only through eyes of faith. Even Jesus said to Nicodemus, "Verily, verily, I say unto thee, Except a man be born again, he cannot see the kingdom of God" (John 3:3).

God's kingdom is as real as the world's kingdoms. It shall last eternally. The nations of the world on the other hand, rise and fall. Their power or size do not guarantee their perma-nence. The state of Rome, whose citizenship many sought, was a powerful ruler of the world, but it has been vanquished. Dur-ing our time, the same has even happened to superpowers. Only the hidden, eternal kingdom of Christ remains.

THE RIGHTS OF CITIZENSHIP

At the change of the millennium, we received a new constitu-tion in Finland. It was distributed to every home. Citizens' rights and responsibilities are defined in the law. We have freedom of religion and freedom of assembly. We have the right to freely choose where to live. This seems self-evident to us, but history tells us that citizens of many nations have lacked this right and many still do. We have the right to participate in political life, by voting, for example. We have compulsory edu-cation and military service. We pay taxes so that organized society can act to our benefit. The rights come with obliga-tions, and the obligations with rights. The right to vote is also an obligation; compulsory education is more of a right.

The constitution also defines the structure of Finnish soci-ety and the hierarchy of the officers of societal duties. First is the President, then the Chairman of the Legislature, the Prime Min-ister, and so on. However, all citizens are equal before the law.

As Christians, we participate in civic affairs. We hold posi-tions of responsibility in the nation and community when they are entrusted to us. We vote in elections and perform duties and functions necessary for society. Scripture teaches us to care for all of the duties given to us as a Christian. "Whatsoever ye do, do it heartily, as to the Lord, and not unto men" (Col. 3:23).

God's kingdom has its own order. A person receives the rights of its citizenship already at birth. It differs from a temporal state in that its citizenship cannot be acquired by application or by joining, but the question is always of birth. A person, who has lost childhood faith and citizenship of heaven receives it through new birth. "Verily, verily, I say unto thee, Except a man be born of water and of the Spirit, he cannot enter the kingdom of God" (John 3:5).

Rank in God's kingdom differs from that of a temporal state. In chapter 18 of the Gospel of Matthew, which we can also call the constitution of God's kingdom, it is related that the disciples were troubled by the question of rank. For that reason, they asked Jesus, "Who is the greatest in the kingdom of Heaven?" Then Jesus took a child, set him in the midst of the disciples, and said, "Verily I say unto you, Except ye be converted, and be as little children, ye shall not enter into the kingdom of heaven. Whosoever therefore shall humble himself as this little child, the same is greatest in the kingdom of heaven" (Matt. 18:2–4).

God's kingdom is a kingdom of children and the childlike. The greatest is the least and the least is the greatest, "Whosoever will be chief among you, let him be your servant" (Matt. 20:27). That is something for us to strive toward, when we also would want to be great and in charge.

God's kingdom is a kingdom of grace and forgiveness. People live there only by grace and forgiveness. If our forgiving attitude ceases, we drift outside the kingdom. Our greatest right as a citizen is forgiveness of sins.

Citizens of God's kingdom also have obligations. The most important, perhaps the only one, is love, because we have become partakers of God's great love. "For this is the message that ye heard from the beginning, that we should love one another" (1 John 3:11). "Beloved, let us love one another: for love is of God; and every one that loveth is born of God, and knoweth God. He that loveth not, knoweth not God; for God is love. In this is manifested God's love toward us, because that God sent his only begotten Son into the world, that we might live through him. Herein is love, not that we loved God, but that he loved us, and sent his Son to be the propitiation for our sins. Beloved, if God so loved us, we ought also to love one another" (1 John 4:7–11).

Love is a caring love. The children of God care for each other, so that no one would drift out of the grace kingdom. In chapter 18 of the Gospel of Matthew, Jesus gives us instruction in this care. They are instructions on caring love, not on ruling or a means for authority. Paul wrote to the Romans, "Wherefore receive ye one another, as Christ also received us, to the glory of God" (Rom. 15:7).

HOW WE DWELL IN TWO KINGDOMS AT THE SAME TIME

Citizenship in two nations creates problems that we cannot resolve by isolating ourselves from the world. It is not God's will, for He has intended that we be connected with other people. Our temporal life is a God-given gift. Our temporal homeland is dear to us. God wishes that we would serve our neighbors as citizens of this land.

Although we dwell in two kingdoms, we must keep them separate. Our [Finnish] national church is not God's kingdom, even if we would have the majority in the Church Council, nor can we care for matters there with majority rule, as they may be cared for in the home Zion. And even if we had the majority on a town council, we would be unable to care for matters according to our wishes, but we would have to take into consideration what the other residents think. If we acted otherwise, the boundary between the two kingdoms, which were intended to be separate, would disappear. Luther warns about this, "For that reason, these two kingdoms must be kept strictly separate from each other and both must be kept in power, one to make people righteous, the other to create outward peace and prevent evil deeds. Neither one is sufficient in this world without the other" (On Earthly Government).

On the other hand, we cannot conduct ourselves in such a way as to behave in our temporal activities as if we were not believing and then, among believers, in their manner. Paul counseled the Corinthians, "Wherefore we labor, that, whether present or absent, we may be accepted of him" (2 Cor. 5:9). In all of our duties, we want to act as God's children. God sends us into the midst of other people to serve them. He wants us to be a light and salt. This does not mean that we should always preach. God's intention is that we would take with us some of that love with which He has loved us, when He has forgiven us all of our sins.

MARRIAGE

Respect for matrimony has crashed in our time. The reason for this has been the general detachment from that set of values whose foundations are in God's Word. At the same time, man has become a shirker of responsibility, a hedonist, and a seeker after his own benefit. In this type of world, a person thinks he doesn't need the security and order in his life that Christian marriage provides.

In the congregation of Christ, the concepts of marriage and family have remained unchanged on a scriptural foundation. Living in this world, however, we are in continual contact with values that oppose the values of God's Word, and they find a sympathetic response in our sin-corrupt hearts. Many persons ponder matters relative to marriage and ask, "Has God really said that?"

COURTING AND ENGAGEMENT

When a child grows into youth, an attraction toward the opposite sex awakens. This is a result of the fact that God created people as male and female. There is nothing wrong and no reason to prevent the attraction of girls to boys and boys to girls. But our time has so overemphasized sexuality, that youth is stripped from many children, and they do not have the opportunity to grow to responsible adulthood. Patience in this area of life is not characteristic of our time, rather one should be able to experience everything immediately. Thus, many are driven into loose human relationships of short duration. Actually, a recently published study indicates that the situation among young people is not as gloomy as one would conclude on the basis of public discussions, literature, and magazines.

Young people get to know each other in life's normal environment. It is completely natural that believing young people seek their future spouse where they meet each other—at services, camps, and *opistos* (folk schools). It is a precious matter when one finds his life-companion from among the believing young people. It is good to get to know each other in the everyday environment. In this way, one is spared from many sad surprises.

Courting is directed toward marriage, so light-minded "flirting" is not appropriate for a believer. In such there is no question of love, or even of infatuation, but of selfish momentary pleasure, which causes sorrow and tears to the courting companion. The matter in consideration is serious enough, that a person who has fallen into this has reason to examine his heart and the foundations of his faith.

Courting, above all, is getting to know one another. When courting companions discuss matters openly, they come to know each other. In this manner, it becomes clear if, on life's important issues, they have such mutual understanding that would form a foundation for lifelong marriage. Many have said that during courtship, especially, they discussed matters of faith. When they noticed that they had a similar understanding about the most important things, it drew them closer and united them. If courting becomes too close physically, the intellectual or emotional familiarization, openness, and closeness suffer. In this way, the courtship is impoverished.

When the young people have become well acquainted and convinced that it is they whom God has intended to join as helpmates for each other, they become engaged. Scripture scarcely speaks of courtship, because, in its culture, parents selected spouses for their children through a spokesman.

Engagement makes the courtship public. It makes known to everyone that the engaged couple intends to marry. Scripture discusses engagement at length. It is used to describe the covenant between Christ and those who believe in Him. Paul reminds the Corinthians that he had served as a spokesman for them, "I have espoused you to one husband, that I may present you as a chaste virgin to Christ" (2 Cor. 11:2). Like this biblical description, the engaged couple promises to be faithful to each other as they await the wedding, the beginning of married life.

Although young people court each other with the right attitude and even get engaged, it can happen that they do not become a married couple. It can become clear, little by little, they are not suited to each other. Separation is painful, but it is not wrong. It is still possible to separate amicably, respecting one another. This possibility no longer exists in marriage.

In spite of the fact that young people court each other with serious intentions, things can happen to them that may remain as burdens on their consciences. "The spirit is willing, but the flesh is weak." If this takes place, it is good to remember, that there is an open fountain in God's congregation for sin and for defilement (Zech. 13:1). It is good if the courting couple together would discuss matters with the confessor.

GOD INSTITUTED MARRIAGE

"So God created man in his own image, in the image of God created he him; male and female created he them. And God blessed them, and God said unto them, Be fruitful and multiply, and replenish the earth" (Gen. 1:27, 28). Scripture relates how mankind was created in God's image as man and woman. Both are crucial to human existence. We are responsible to God and created to live together with each other. Unity is realized most deeply between spouses. The description of Creation illustrates this, "Therefore shall a man leave his father and his mother, and shall cleave unto his wife: and they shall be one flesh" (Gen. 2:24).

The relationship between a man and a woman includes both emotional and physical unity. The woman was created to be a helpmeet for the man (Gen. 2:18). I have read that the Hebrew word in question means "help that is facing you." Spouses are equals and can examine themselves in each other as in a mirror. Their mutual life contains the whole richness of life. Because of the fall into sin, however, it can never be realized as illustrated in the Creation narrative. For that reason, we need the gospel, which is the great treasure and source of strength of a believing home.

MARRIAGE IS LIFELONG

The Pharisees came to Jesus to argue about divorce and referred to Moses, who had allowed a man to write a bill of divorcement to put away his wife (Deut. 24:1). Then Jesus answered, "For the hardness of your heart he wrote you this precept. But from the beginning of the creation God made them male and female. For this cause shall a man leave his father and mother, and cleave to his wife; and they twain shall be one flesh: so then they are no more twain, but one flesh. What therefore God hath joined together, let not man put asunder" (Mark 10:5–9).

Therefore, although the courts may grant a divorce and, in this manner, undo a covenant that was once made, the marriage shall still remain in force before the face of God. Already, during the Old Testament, Prophet Malachi rebuked the people for breaking their marriages (Mal. 2:14–16).

According to Matthew, in Jesus' discussion with the Pharisees, He allowed divorce because of adultery (Matt. 5:31–32). Luther discusses this matter in his writing regarding marriage. He points out that adultery is a sin onto death. According to Mosaic Law, a person who broke the marriage vows was to be stoned to death (Lev. 20:10). On the other hand, however, Jesus did not approve the stoning of an adulteress (John 8:3–11), but forgiveness was greater than the Law.

A couple of decades ago, divorce was discussed at length at a speakers' meeting. At that time, the speaker-brothers held to the above mentioned quotation from the Gospel of Mark. Marriage is lifelong: what God has joined, let not man put asunder. This does not lessen the seriousness of the sin of adultery, but provides an opportunity for a person to return, repent, and receive forgiveness for a grievous transgression.

LUTHER'S TEACHINGS ON MATRIMONY

Luther did not consider matrimony to be a sacrament in the manner of the Catholic Church. He also fought against celibacy for the clergy and considered the vows of monks and nuns to be against God's will. In his manuscript, "On Matrimony," he states that God's Word, "Be fruitful and multiply," is not a commandment, but a godly deed. Obstructing or neglecting it is not within our power. It is just as unavoidable as that a man is in existence, and more unavoidable than eating and drinking, keeping one's body clean, sleeping or staying awake. It is nature planted into a person. Luther continues later, "The world says of matrimony: 'short joy, long regret.' But say what it wishes, for what God creates and wills, that is an object for it to mock....Solomon says, 'Whoso findeth a wife findeth a good thing'" (Prov. 18:22). They who understand this, firmly believe that God has instituted matrimony, put man and woman together, and ordained the bearing and care of children. They have God's Word regarding this (Gen. 1:28).

Luther writes in the Large Catechism that the Sixth Commandment has been directed especially toward those who are married. "Let us carefully note, first, how highly God honors and glorifies the married life, sanctioning and protecting it by his commandment. He sanctioned it above in the fourth commandment, 'You shall honor father and mother; but here, as I said, he has secured it and protected it. Therefore he also wishes us to honor, maintain, and cherish it as a divine and blessed estate. Significantly he established it as the first of all institutions, and he created man and woman differently (as is evident) not for lewdness but to be true to each other, be fruitful, beget children, and support and bring them up to the glory of God."

The Everyday Characteristics of Marriage

In marriage, couples continue to learn the art of living together throughout their lives. As selfishness is part of our nature, it does not naturally follow that two persons will adapt to living together "as one flesh." In everyday life's many forms, the dissimilarities of the spouses are felt. Difficulties also are encountered there. When differences of opinion arise and arguments raise their heads, it is easy to forget what was once promised "before the face of God and in the presence of the congregation."

"Who's the boss at our house?" is a vain and wrong question. It is the same question that the disciples presented, "Who is greatest among us?" By saying, "The Son of man came not to be ministered unto, but to minister" (Mark 10:45), Jesus set himself as the example for the disciples, who were quarreling about their positions.

Scripture counsels, "Wives, submit yourselves unto your own husbands, as unto the Lord. For the husband is the head of the wife, even as Christ is the head of the church: and he is the saviour of the body. Therefore, as the church is subject unto Christ, so let the wives be to their own husbands in every thing" (Eph. 5:22–24). In the same manner, Scripture counsels, "Husbands, love your wives, even as Christ also loved the church, and gave himself for it (Eph. 5:25). This advice shifts the question of authority and of station aside. Serving each other replaces it. In speaking of the husband being the head of the wife, the Greek New Testament uses the same word as the point of a plow, which receives the bumps and the blows when cultivating. The word, which is often referred to, now receives broader content. To be the head means to protect and support.

Both spouses have their own duties determined by gender. However, we cannot make a pattern that, as such, would adapt to every marriage. The pattern of living in a home is determined by the weaknesses and strengths of the members of the home. The most important thing is that they compete in honoring one another (Rom. 12:10).

Conservative Laestadian families are often known for their numerous children. Probably no other factor connected to our lives or teachings has drawn so much attention from outsiders. In this matter, we also experience heavy pressure from the world. Scripture does not teach family planning, but it guides us to regard children as God's gifts (Ps. 127:3–5). When He created man and woman, God said, "Multiply, and replenish the earth" (Gen. 1:28). The understanding of the believers in this matter is based on God's Word. We think as Luther did, "I believe that God has created me and all other creatures." Children bring difficulties and work to the family, but also God's rich blessing. Life feels worth living, when it has the content that God intended.

The Great Mystery of Marriage

When he gave advice to spouses, Paul compared matrimony to the fellowship of Christ and His congregation. These analogies to submission, faithfulness, and all-sacrificing love strip us of our false notions of personal privilege, selfish entitlement, and success. On the other hand, they give the foundations to marriage that will last through changing times and amid turmoil. They give marriage a special sanctity and join the spouses more closely, as well as bring the gospel of the glory of Christ to everyday trials and temptations. In a believing home, there is an open fountain against sin and defilement. The believing home is God's kingdom in miniature and a part of the large family of God.

OUR RESPONSIBILITY FOR TEMPORAL TALENTS

GIFTS INCLUDE RESPONSIBILITY

Jesus related a parable about a master, some servants, and talents, which the master had entrusted to them (Matt. 25:14–30). The master is God, the servants are people, and the talents are the gifts that God has given them.

The parable teaches us that the gifts have responsibility attached to their use. God did not give them just for our own joy and benefit, but also so that his purposes would be fulfilled in our lives. The master trusted his servants and gave them great freedom in their actions but did not free them from responsibility. Freedom and responsibility are part of a person's life. The greater the freedom, the greater the responsibility. Responsibility separates man from other creatures.

God gave the rest of creation into man's care (Gen. 1:26). In this portion of the creation narrative, man's freedom and responsibility are described perhaps the most broadly. God did not give man the right to spoil and destroy nature or the rest of creation, but he called man to assist Him in cultivating and caring for the earth. What will we answer as members of mankind, when once we will be asked how we have taken care of this duty? Our heads will probably drop down, and we will not be able to defend ourselves with anything. Selfishness, greed, and shortsighted pursuit of one's own benefit have destroyed that which we should have tended.

In the parable, the master gave varying amounts of talents, but all received at least one. The talent, as it is translated in the New [Finnish] Church Bible, was a very large coin. It equaled 6,000 denarii, and one denarius was the regular daily wage for a man. One talent, therefore, equaled approximately what a workman could earn during his lifetime. We could also consider that the talent, which all of the servants received for their use, was their temporal life. Every person is responsible for his life, independent of whether he is conscious of it or not.

God has equipped us for the sake of living. In the Small Catechism, Luther explains the First Article of The Creed, "I believe that God has made me and all other creatures; that he has given and still preserves to me my body and soul, eyes, ears, and all my members, my reason and all my senses." God does not "clone." He has not created two identical persons, but rather every person is an individual. God has His purpose and plan for every person. He has given everyone precisely those gifts necessary to realize that purpose.

We often trivialize our own gifts and are jealous of the gifts of others. Sometimes, on the other hand, we overvalue our own abilities and skills. The cause of both behaviors is our own pride. We would want to be better than others. However, God's Word exhorts us to reasonably value ourselves and our gifts (Rom. 12:3). Sometimes we turn down a duty offered us, thinking, "Let others who have better gifts do it." Are we then like that servant, who received one talent and buried it in the ground?

PEOPLE WERE CREATED TO BE WITH EACH OTHER

The gifts, which God has given us, also include those close to us. God did not create people to be alone but to be together. God's statement, "It is not good that man should be alone" (Gen. 2:18), primarily means a spouse in marriage, but it also covers the family circle, all other people, and interaction with them. Our responsibility for the gifts that God has given us includes our relationship to our neighbors. God's Word guides us to love our neighbors and to act in their best interest. Living together with other people gives purpose and content to our lives, while loneliness and selfishness bring distress and emptiness.

When we work with other people and in their best interest, we can use our God-given gifts as He has intended. However, connection with other people brings not only content and good fortune into our lives, but often problems, as well. When we do not know how we should act, we can remember from the Sermon on the Mount Jesus' advice known as the Golden Rule: "Whatsoever ye would that men should do unto you, do ye even so to them: for this is the law and the prophets" (Matt. 7:12).

We have a tendency to limit the circle to which our neighborly love extends. We are similar to the scribe, who asked Jesus, "Who is my neighbor?" (Luke 10:29). The person, who asked the question, probably had his own answer ready: his neighbors were the Jews, and the closest among them were those who followed the Mosaic Law as interpreted by the scribes and the Pharisees. The Gentiles, sinners, and publicans were left outside this man's love toward his neighbor. Jesus answered his question with the familiar parable of the Good Samaritan and concluded His teaching with the words, "Go and do thou likewise." In His Sermon on the Mount, Jesus extended the love toward our neighbor to include even our enemies.

In Luther's time, the Catholic Church had developed in such a way that spiritual and temporal life were separate from each other. Luther opposed justification by works, as well as shutting God out of temporal life. To him, the workday life had been intended and given by God. The concept of a continuously active God and a living, ever-present Christ characterized

Luther's framework of thought. Luther's concept of Scripture rises from this foundation. To him, Creation and Redemption were not two separate matters, but he looked at Creation in the light of Redemption. Justification by faith is the foundation. When God justifies a person alone by faith, alone by grace, and alone by the merit of Christ, a person is freed to serve his neighbor. Faith is weighed by our everyday life.

WORK IS A GOD-GIVEN DUTY

Work is a duty that God has given to man; therein He has hidden His blessing. Work includes responsibility, whether we do the work in someone's employ or as an independent entrepreneur. The greater our freedom, the greater our responsibility. Paul advised the Christians of his time, "Servants, be obedient to them that are your masters according to the flesh, with fear and trembling, in singleness of your heart, as unto Christ; not with eyeservice, as menpleasers; but as the servants of Christ, doing the will of God from the heart; with good will doing service, as to the Lord, and not to men" (Eph. 6:5–7). He continued, "Masters, give unto your servants that which is just and equal; knowing that ye also have a Master in heaven" (Col. 4:1). These admonitions from God's Word also apply to today's work life.

We do not perform work only for our daily bread, but also because we serve our neighbors and are God's work companions, His subordinates, in governing this temporal world. To Luther, work was part of the calling. Because of the deep significance of work, unemployment is a difficult problem. Unemployment assistance only partially removes the detrimental effects of joblessness. However, there is reason to remember that our worth as a person is not measured by how productive we are or how great an income our work produces. If we think incorrectly in this, we do not remember that, in Jesus' parable, the servants each received a different number of talents. Even when unemployed, we can do beneficial work and work in the calling that God gives.

EDUCATION IS A GIFT FROM GOD

We live in an education-minded society. Earlier, education was the privilege of only a few and the period for education was strictly limited. When one's education ended, the student was ready for his vocation, which he practiced until he retired. It is different now. An education is everyone's right, more time is used in getting it, and it is continuing. Because of the changes in society, and production, new duties and vocations are born, and, at the same time, the old vocations may become obsolete. Retraining is necessary.

It is not self-evident that everyone experiences education as a gift and a privilege. Sometimes, it may feel that it is a waste of time and a hindrance. One may want to get straight to work to earn money to fulfill needs and hopes that seem so important. Such thinking is shortsighted. During our youth, studying is often the work and duty that God has intended for us. Through it, we obtain the knowledge and skills which we will need later. We cannot measure an education's value only by how well-paying a job we can get with it. Even if earnings do not grow, education broadens our intellectual horizons and enriches our lives. When I think of my own life and studies, it is almost humorous to note that the so-called professional subjects have provided me only limited benefit. Instead, the liberal arts courses have been many times more beneficial to me than I thought in my youth. I regret my laziness in studying foreign languages.

Study also brings out the varied gifts of different measure that God has given us. Responsibility increases with one's gifts. If we have received abundantly, we do not have reason to be proud, for the gifts have been given by God. If we feel that we have received fewer gifts, they also can be developed. God has not left anyone without gifts, nor has anyone received too few gifts. It doesn't pay to leave our gifts unused, in other words, it doesn't pay to bury our talent in the ground.

Often, the place where we want to study does not open for us, although we may apply several times. It is difficult to be satisfied with this and to apply elsewhere. It is difficult to give up dreams, especially when they are genuine and well-founded. Even in these situations, it is good to remember that

God leads our lives in more detail than we notice. I have experienced this, myself. When I have understood the matter in retrospect, there has been reason to thank God for the doors that He has closed, and for those that He has opened.

When the master arrived, he called the servants to account for themselves. Those, who had taken care of their talents in the manner that the master intended, were called to His joy. On the other hand, that servant, who had hidden his talent in the ground, lost that too. The parable makes us accountable for the use of our own gifts. Responsibility and accountability are matters that can easily oppress us. We feel that we have neglected the care of the talents entrusted to us.

The correct care of the talents is the same as bearing fruit. So that we would understand what is under consideration, we have reason to remember the teaching of Jesus about the vine and its branches, "Abide in me, and I in you. As the branch cannot bear fruit of itself, except it abide in the vine; no more can ye, except ye abide in me" (John 15:4). The question is not that we be skilled and accomplish much, but that we would be partakers of Christ through faith. When we can remain as living branches in Christ, the Vine, God can accomplish His own purpose in our lives. Even for us it becomes true what Paul said of his activities as a worker in God's kingdom and as the apostle to the Gentiles, "Yet not I, but the grace of God which was with me" (1 Cor. 15:10). The reward, which the master gives his servants, is the reward of grace.

THE LORD OF TIME AND
TIME-BOUND MAN

AT THE CHANGE OF THE MILLENNIUM

The change of millennia included suspense, and made people stop to think of the past and to ask about the future. It was an event, which only a small portion of mankind has been able to experience. After the change of the prior millennium, 30–40 generations have lived without coming even close to that milepost. Many certainly even gave thought to what is time and what is eternity, that dimension where time doesn't exist. A millennium is such a long period of time that when it changes, eternity touches man, who is shackled to time.

During the few weeks prior to the change of millennia, the newspaper in my hometown interviewed people of different ages and educational backgrounds. They were asked whom they considered the most remarkable persons of the concluding millennium and what, in their opinion, were the most important events and noteworthy inventions of that period of time. Naturally, the answers differed, but they had a common trait. Nearly everything important had happened, all noteworthy persons had lived, and the great inventions had been invented during the past fifty years. Only a few things of importance had taken place during the first half of the last century, in the previous century, or before that.

The sampling, which included over a hundred people, shows how we are tied to our own time. Although we might already be old, our memory does not cover more than a small fraction of the past millennium. We must take information from history to assist our memories to recall what happened during the past millennium. Even historical information becomes more meager the nearer we come to the beginning of another era.

In a similar manner, the newspaper asked people about their concept of the future at the change of millennia. The answers gave a picture of people's hopes and fears. Again, they had a common characteristic. The period of time, to which the expectations extended, was only a few years. We do not have the ability to see into the future. The speed of change makes it more difficult to evaluate the future. People are, indeed all of mankind is, bound to time.

Man Bound to Time and the Lord of Time

A healthy person can move. If he loses his ability to move about, or if it is limited because of illness or an injury, he experiences it as a trial. We can move north and south, east and west. We can climb and descend. We have these three dimensions at our disposal. The question is of something so natural that we seldom think of it.

The fourth dimension is time. It differs from the above-mentioned dimensions because it is not in our control. We cannot move freely through time, but we are bound to it. Time moves on, and we move with it. Sometimes time flies, and sometimes, it crawls. At other times, it feels that it has stopped for a moment. We cannot hasten the passage of time, or turn it back. We cannot jump forward or past a difficult period at hand. Time is part of our lives so fundamentally, that it is difficult to imagine a state of being in which time does not exist. Such is eternity. Luther illustrates this by describing a small bird, which flies to a mountain and scrapes its beak on it and flies away. After a millennium, it returns and does the same thing. Sometime, after an incomprehensible length of time, the mountain is worn down. But eternity never ends. A thousand years is not eternity, not even a fraction of it, even though, at its change, it makes us consider eternity.

To people born into and bound to time, Scripture speaks of God, Who is not bound to time. He, the Creator of heaven and earth, is also the Lord of time. He has set time to perform its function and has created man into this time. He has created man to be an eternal being also. He has intended man to live even after time no longer exists.

GOD'S TIME AND MAN'S TIME

God has always existed. He has neither beginning nor end, and time does not bind Him. Even the fourth dimension is freely in His use. He is also unchanging, for change belongs to time. God has His own time. It is not the same as man's time. It cannot be measured with our clocks or calendars.

Once, in eternity, there was the moment when God started His Creation. It was His time. With His Word, He created the earth and all that we see and comprehend. He also created all that which we do not see, understand, or comprehend. He established the laws and order of nature. He has not needed to correct or revise them. They are in force until God's time, which is the last day, comes. No one else knows that day but the Father alone.

God established the borders of time for the world. He created man into time, but differentiated him from the rest of creation. He made man an eternal being. God created man both for time and eternity. For that reason, that, which is outside the realm of time, is of interest to every person. On a clear autumn evening, many of us have looked at the starry sky and thought as did the psalmist, "When I consider thy heavens, the work of thy fingers, the moon and the stars, which thou hast ordained; what is man, that thou art mindful of him? And the son of man, that thou visitest him?" (Ps. 8:3,4).

The future has not been veiled to the Lord of Time as it is to us people. He even knew that man would fall into sin. The Son promised to redeem man, who would fall into the power of sin and death. God created everything dependent upon the promise given by the Son. Redemption existed from the beginning and brought the possibility of eternal life within reach of fallen man. The following words from Psalms convey to us a portion of the discussion between the Father and the Son. The Father turns to the Son and says, "Thou art my Son; this day have I begotten thee. Ask of me, and I shall give thee the heathen for thine inheritance, and the uttermost parts of the earth for thy possession" (Ps. 2:7,8). To this the Son answers, "I delight to do thy will, O my God" (Ps. 40:8).

The Son, Christ, existed for a long time among men only as the Word of the Promise. They, who believed the Promise, awaited its fulfillment. They probably thought that God tarried long. However, He did not tarry, not even to try the faith of the children of God of the Old Covenant. His time had not yet come.

But then God's time came. The angels appeared to the shepherds and announced that a Savior had been born unto them. The angels and the whole heavenly host praised God, "Glory to God in the highest, and on earth peace, good will toward men" (Luke 2:14). John says at the beginning of his Gospel, "And the Word was made flesh, and dwelt among us, (and we beheld his glory, the glory as of the only begotten of the Father,) full of grace and truth" (John 1:14). "But when the fulness of the time was come, God sent forth his Son, made of a woman, made under the law, to redeem them that were under the law, that we might receive the adoption of sons" (Gal. 4:4,5).

It was God's time when Jesus began His public ministry. Mark writes of it, "Now after that John was put in prison, Jesus came into Galilee, preaching the gospel of God's kingdom, and saying, The time is fulfilled, and the kingdom of God is at hand: repent ye, and believe the gospel" (Mark 1:14,15).

Luke tells of the turning point of Jesus' public ministry, "And it came to pass, when the time was come that he should be received up, he steadfastly set his face to go to Jerusalem" (Luke 9:51). It was time for Jesus to redeem His promise, which He had given to the Father before the beginning of time. God purposefully fulfilled His salvation plan, without delaying or hastening.

God's time is not only linked to the great events of salvation history; even we can observe in the happenings of God's kingdom when it is, or has been, God's time. Precisely this was in question when, to our surprise, new doors opened over a decade ago for the work of the gospel outside the boundaries of our nation [Finland]. Thirty years earlier, foreign mission work had risen as a topic of dissension. The question is not of the principle, for we had the clear word of Jesus, "Go ye into all the world, and preach the gospel to every creature" (Mark 16:15). The disagreement regarded joining the activities of the Finnish Mission Society. Conservative Laestadians turned down the offer for mutual work, but agreed on the importance of mission work and remained waiting for the time when God would provide opportunity for their own mission work. This position was held in spite of accusations and criticism. God's time came thirty years later.

God's time also touches the individual. It is God's time when He awakens the conscience and allows His kingdom to approach. It is then possible to repent and to believe the gospel. "Behold, now is the accepted time; now is the day of salvation" (2 Cor. 6:2). A person cannot repent when it feels convenient for him, but only then when it is God's time. For that reason, it is a serious matter when a person hears the call from God's kingdom. The person who rejects the call doesn't know if God's time will come again. Neither does he know when his time of grace will end or when his day of departure will come. God, alone, knows this; He has known the number of our days already before our birth. "Thine eyes did see my substance, yet being unperfect; and in thy book all my members were written, which in continuance were fashioned, when as yet there was none of them" (Ps. 139:16).

MEASURING TIME

Man has an understanding of time. There exist at least two differing concepts of time. The cyclical concept has its origins in Greece's Hellenistic culture. According to this concept, time's movement is circular. According to the linear concept, time progresses as it were a straight line, it has a beginning as well as an end point. This concept originates in Judaism, and has moved from there into the realm of the Christian faith. The Christian concept of time is based on scriptural revelation that the time of man has a beginning and an end. The present moment divides time into two parts, the past and the future. It is like a fleet arrow, on which we move forward.

In order to live and function in time, where to God has bound him, man has developed methods to measure time. God gave the foundations for this already in Creation. When the earth revolved once around the sun, a year had passed. Nature's activity revealed the changes of the seasons. When the moon circled the earth once, a month had passed. Its passage could be followed by the shape of the moon. When the earth rotated once on its axis, a day had passed. At the same time the day's different parts were born: morning, afternoon, evening, and night. Man could follow the passage of the day by the height and direction of the sun. In the beginning, there were no clocks, but man learned early to measure the passage of time using the sun's shadow to his benefit.

Scripture describes the sundial of Ahaz. Prophet Isaiah revealed to King Hezekiah that God would heal him of a serious illness and that he did not have to die yet. Hezekiah asked for a sign to verify God's promise. Isaiah answered that the shadow on the sundial of Ahaz would move back ten degrees for a sign that he would be healed. Hezekiah easily understood that the shadow moves clockwise, but it was difficult to comprehend backward movement of the shadow (2 Kings 20:9–11). Hezekiah, himself, had experienced that time was not in man's control. It was just as difficult for him to understand, as it is for us, that time and the laws of nature are ruled by God. It is a blessed and marvelous thing that the Sun of Grace moves counterclockwise and wipes away previously committed sins.

When God had created the earth, He rested and sanctified the seventh day to be the day of rest. In this manner, the week was born. Its passage could not be followed like the day and the month from nature or the heavenly bodies. The week had another purpose. God knew that man, whom He had created, also needed a day of rest. The stressed people of our time would feel better if the sanctification of the day of rest were not so commonly forgotten. The weekly day of rest is not only for idleness or hobbies, but also for hearing God's Word. Luther explains the third commandment in the Small Catechism, "We should so fear and love God as not to despise preaching and His Word, but deem it holy, and willingly hear and learn it." In the Large Catechism, Luther states his thought, "The emphasis of this commandment is not on resting, but on sanctifying."

It was easy to follow the passage of time for one revolution of the sun, but memory and life extended further. A need to observe time, or the calendar, was born. At least two problems had to be resolved: Where would the observation of years be started, and, what would be done since one revolution of the sun was not exactly twelve months long? The differences were not remarkable during a period of a few years, but if longer periods were considered, the more problematic they became.

Different nations resolved the problems in different ways. History relates of many kinds of calendars, which have been made more accurate and changed. At present, one uniform calendar system is probably in use in nearly the entire world. The difficulties, that have been experienced in the observation of time, show that managing time is difficult for man.

Determining a time by the ruler in power was formerly common. Prophet Isaiah begins the story of his repentance in this manner, "In the year that king Uzziah died I saw also the Lord sitting upon a throne, high and lifted up" (Isa. 6:1). This determination of time shows especially clearly when Luke at the beginning of his Gospel, ties the births and public ministry of John the Baptist and Jesus, to the Julian calendar: "There was in the days of Herod, the king of Judea, a certain priest named Zechariah, of the course of Abijah: and his wife was of the daughters of Aaron, and her name was Elizabeth" (Luke 1:5). "And it came to pass in those days, that there went out a decree from Caesar Augustus, that all the world should be taxed. (And this taxing was first made when Cyrenius was governor of Syria.)" (Luke 2:1, 2). "Now in the fifteenth year of the reign of Tiberius Caesar, Pontius Pilate being governor of Judea, and Herod being tetrarch of Galilee, and his brother Philip tetrarch of Itruraea and of the region of Trachonitis, and Lysanias the tetrarch of Abilene" (Luke 3:1).

The practice of keeping Christ's birth as the starting point for counting time became general in France and Germany in the 900s. This practice is presently common even in those countries where Christianity is the religion of only a small minority.

THE LAST TIMES

The end of the millennium stimulated some unsound speculation and expectations. People wanted to determine appointed times and draw conclusions from scriptural prophecies that had been taken out of context. They were found to be wrong. There is reason to stay away from such calculations. As historical and as serious a matter as the end of a millennium is, it still is only a brief moment, whose time is determined by the unsure human measure of time. God has not bound himself to our calendar.

The early congregation lived awaiting Christ's quick return. Had He not promised to come a second time in His glory? It is related in the Acts of the Apostles how the Christians sold their houses and possessions and everything was held in common. When Christ's coming was delayed, the people who waited for Him had problems. Is Christ even coming? The Christians of that period were just as bound to time as we are.

It appears that in Corinth and Thessalonica an understanding arose that they who had died before Christ's coming had believed in vain. Paul refuted this, "Now if Christ be preached that he rose from the dead, how say some among you that there is no resurrection of the dead?" (1 Cor. 15:12). He wrote to the Thessalonians, "But I would not have you to be ignorant, brethren, concerning them which are asleep, that ye sorrow not, even as others which have no hope. For if we believe that Jesus died and rose again, even so them also which sleep in Jesus will God bring with him" (1 Thess. 4:13,14). The gospel, which they who had slept in faith had heard, had made them partakers in Christ's Resurrection. When the last day dawns and the graves open, they shall rise to meet Christ together with all believers. The time of waiting will not have felt long to them. Time lost its hold on them when they closed their eyes to this world.

Peter wrote that a thousand years with the Lord is as one day (2 Pet. 3:8). He did not mean that we should take the phrase as a unit of measure by which we would observe God's time, and thereby try to fit His omnipotence into our limited comprehension. Peter's words teach us the very opposite that God's time is different from man's, and it is not for man to measure. That word was written for the people who awaited a quick coming of the Lord. They doubted when His coming was delayed. The doubts were increased when some gave up believing, waiting, and watching, and started to ridicule. Peter especially emphasized that the Lord will come unexpectedly, "as a thief in the night." He says that the coming tarries because there are yet those who must come in.

The New Testament also speaks of the last times or days, as well as the events and signs of the times preceding the coming of Christ. In the revelation about the last times, two matters are intertwined. First of all, the children of God are warned about the dangers and errors of the last times, and the importance of watchfulness is emphasized, for the last day shall come unexpectedly. Paul wrote to the Corinthians, "Now all these things happened to them for ensamples: and they are written for our admonition, upon whom the ends of the world are come" (1 Cor. 10:11). The Epistle to the Hebrews starts, "God, who at sundry times and in divers manners spake in time past unto the fathers by the prophets, hath in these last days spoken unto us by his Son" (Heb. 1:1,2).

The writers comprehended through faith that the last phase of God's salvation plan, which He had laid down before the beginning of the ages, had begun. Paul joins in this thought with his words to the Corinthians, "God was in Christ, reconciling the world unto himself, not imputing their trespasses unto them; and hath committed unto us the word of reconciliation" (2 Cor. 5:19). The Father created and the Son redeemed. When the Redemption had taken place, the congregation of the New Testament, having received the office of the Holy Spirit, set out to bear the sermon of reconciliation into all the world.

In his Gospel, Matthew preserved Jesus' own teachings about the last times (Matt. 24,25). The signs are evident in both the outward and spiritual worlds. They are also in God's kingdom. Nevertheless, Christ will come unexpectedly. Ordinary workday life will continue until the end. On the day that Christ will come, two persons will be sowing or harvesting in the field, one will be taken and the other left. Two persons will be grinding grain into flour, one will be taken and the other left. "But of that day and hour knoweth no man, no, not the angels of heaven, but my Father only" (Matt. 24:36). All of the scriptural teachings regarding the last times are dominated by the admonition to watch and the warning against being led astray. We want to believe so that we will be ready to receive Christ. Ahead of us is a journey on which we will depart unexpectedly.

God's kingdom is secure. When fatigue weighs heavily, the children of God admonish each other to watch. The apostle exhorted the Hebrews, who were also troubled by fatigue, "And let us consider one another to provoke unto love and to good works: not forsaking the assembling of ourselves together, as the manner of some is; but exhorting one another: and so much the more, as ye see the day approaching" (Heb. 10:24, 25). Caring love works to the end so that the weak and tired will reach the destination. The Lord Jesus is the throne of grace until He moves to the throne of glory. "Lo, I am with you alway, even unto the end of the world" (Matt. 28:20).

ETERNAL LIFE

WHEN TIME WILL NOT EXIST

Busyness and the feeling that there isn't enough time is characteristic of our time, whereas in eternity, time will have ceased to exist entirely. Then, all the clocks will have stopped, and no one will be tearing pages from a calendar. No one will be in a hurry. Although time-schackled man has difficulty comprehending eternity, it has always fascinated him and occupied his mind. The understanding that when the shackles of time are broken, death loses its grip on him, has heightened man's interest.

SCRIPTURE'S REVELATION ABOUT ETERNAL LIFE

The Triune God is eternal. He has neither beginning nor end. "The Father is eternal, the Son is eternal, the Holy Spirit is eternal" (The Athanasian Creed). Isaiah prophesies about Christ's birth," For unto us a child is born, unto us a son is given: and the government shall be upon his shoulder: and his name shall be called Wonderful, Counselor, The mighty God, The everlasting Father, The Prince of Peace" (Isa. 9:6).

Only God has life in His control. When God spoke to Moses from the burning bush and sent him to be the leader of His people, Moses asked God for His name. God answered, "Thus shalt thou say unto the children of Israel, I AM hath sent me unto you" (Exod. 3:14). Only God can name himself in this manner, for only He has life and only He can give life. Unless God gives life, no one can say, "I am."

God created man in His own image. He gave man life and made of him an eternal being. The God-given life was eternal. Man lost this gift in the Fall into sin and came under the power of death. The Son also had life as the Father did, as He, himself, states, "For as the Father hath life in himself; so hath he given to the Son to have life in himself" (John 5:26). By His redemption work, Christ reopened the broken connection to life. "God hath given to us eternal life, and this life is in his Son. He that hath the Son hath life; and he that hath not the Son of God hath not life" (1 John 5:11,12).

The believing person lives eternal life already in time, but looks at it as if through a mirror. Only when he has reached the destination, will he actually comprehend how great a gift Christ has merited for him. "But the God of all grace, who hath called us unto his eternal glory by Christ Jesus, after that ye have suffered a while, make you perfect, stablish, strengthen, settle you. To him be glory and dominion for ever and ever. Amen" (1 Pet. 5:10,11).

Scripture speaks much about the reality of eternal life, but little about what eternal life is like. No one, who has reached the destination, has returned to relate to us about it. The rich man, having gone to torment, hoped that Lazarus would be sent to relate to his brothers about the importance of repentance, but this did not happen (Luke 16:19–31). Isaiah states instead that, God, himself, excepted, no one has heard or seen what happens to those who wait for the Lord (Isa. 64:4).

Paul, nevertheless, wrote the words to the Corinthians that have been quoted often and applied to heavenly joy, "Eye hath not seen, nor ear heard, neither have entered into the heart of man, the things which God hath prepared for them that love him. But God hath revealed them unto us by his Spirit: for the Spirit searcheth all things, yea, the deep things of God" (1 Cor. 2:9,10). In spite of the similarity of the words, Paul did not quote the previous quotation from Isaiah, but, according to the church father Origen, from the revelation of Elijah, which has been left out of the canon of the Old Testament. Paul apparently did not mean with his quotation the beauty of heaven, but the grace kingdom upon earth, which can be seen only through faith. On the other hand, the Spirit reveals to us that it will be good to be in heaven.

LUTHER'S THOUGHTS

In his book, In the Battles of Life, Luther relates that, when he was gravely ill during 1537–1538, he pondered eternal life. He did not fear death, but left himself and his life in God's hands. He was sure that he already owned eternal life, for he believed in Christ. During his illness, he spoke many beautiful words about the life to come and its unspeakable joy, which the human mind, however, cannot comprehend.

Neither did Luther know when God will create a new heaven and a new earth. He was of that opinion that we should not even ask for that knowledge, since we do not even comprehend the first creation, though we have seen nature and studied it. He pondered how one can get time to pass in eternity as there will not be change or work. Then he realized that there would be enough to study for all of eternity when God opens His secrets. To support his concept, he took Philip's plea, "Lord, show us the Father, and it sufficeth us" (John 14:8).

Once Luther pondered with his family and friends whether they would know each other in heaven. He answered favorably to the pondering, since Adam knew Eve when he awoke from his sleep, although he had not met her before. Adam did not ask, "Where did you come from?" He realized, "This is now bone of my bones and flesh of my flesh." Luther supported his understanding, "Adam was full of the Holy Spirit, and he had the true recognition of God. We will be renewed into this sense and image of God in our coming life in Christ, so that we will know our father and mother and each other better, as Adam knew Eve."

SIN AND DEATH ARE GONE

If this temporal world created by God is good, although sin has badly corrupted it, how good then will be the new heaven and new earth, where righteousness dwells. Sin and death shall be gone; pain, suffering, and distress will be gone. Joy, peace, and love will be present permanently. The sun and the moon, "the timekeepers," will no longer be seen. They won't be needed, when Christ, himself will be as the sun. What more could we wish for! It pays to believe.

"For, behold, I create new heavens and a new earth: and the former shall not be remembered, nor come into mind. But be ye glad and rejoice for ever in that which I create: for, behold, I create Jerusalem a rejoicing, and her people a joy. And I will rejoice in Jerusalem, and joy in my people: and the voice of weeping shall be no more heard in her, nor the voice of crying" (Isa. 65:17–19).

REFERENCE WORKS

The Holy Bible (King James Version)
(Some quotations are translated from the Finnish Church Bible)

Evankelis-luterilaisen kirkon tunnustuskirjat. Jyväskylä 1990

The Confessional Articles of the Evangelical Lutheran Church. Jyväskylä 1990

Luther, Martti
Valitut teokset. Porvoo 1958–1959.
Luther CD-ROM:iin sisältyvä kirjallisuus. 1996

Luther, Martin
Selected Works. Porvoo 1958–1959.
Literature by Luther on CD-ROM. 1996

Kristinoppi
Hyväksytty Suomen kuudennessatoista varsinaisessa kirkolliskokouksessa vuonna 1948. Pieksämäki 1988.

Christian Doctrine
Approved in 1948 at the Finnish Sixteenth Regular Church Council.
Pieksämäki 1988 (English translations by Jon Bloomquist and Paul Sorvo)

Huovinen, Eero (toim.) (Ed.)
Martti Luther: Kaste ja usko. Jyväskylä 1991
Martin Luther: Baptism and Faith. Jyväskylä 1991

Kinnunen, Pekka
Kristus on Raamatun Herra ja Kuningas. Jyväskylä 1983.
Christ is the Lord and King of the Bible. Jyväskylä 1983.

Laulaja, Jorma
Elämän oikea ja väärä. Juva 1994
The Right and Wrong of Life. Juva 1994

Mannermaa, Tuomo
Kaksi rakkautta. Juva 1983
Two Loves. Juva 1983

Niinivaara, Erkki
Maallinen ja Hengellinen. Porvoo 1952
The Secular and the Spiritual. Porvoo 1952

Ott, Heinrich
Jumala. Pieksämäki 1978
God. Pieksämäki 1978

Palva, Heikki
Raamatun tietosanasto. Juva 1995
Dictionary of Bible Knowledge. Juva 1995

Pinomaa, Lennart
Voittava usko. Porvoo 1972.
Victorious Faith. Porvoo 1972

Reinikainen, Erkki
Lisää meille uskoa. Jyväskylä 1969
Myrskyt lakkaavat. Jyväskylä 1983.
Näin on kirjoitettu. Jyväskylä 1986.
Näin on uskottu. Jyväskylä 1990
Niin kuin kuvastimesta. Jyväskylä 1994

Reinikainen, Erkki
  Increase Our Faith
  The Storms Will Cease
  So It Has Been Written
  So It Has Been Believed
  As Through a Mirror

SRK:n vuosikirjat 1984–2000. Jyväskylä 1985–2000

SRK Yearbooks 1984–2000. Jyväskylä 1985–2000

Christmas 2004